P9-BII-585

Living Grace

How grace affects your whole life

Volume 1

"Building a culture of grace"

Living Grace

Copyright © New Nature Publications
ISBN: 978-988-16029-1-6

Published in 2012 by New Nature Publications. All rights reserved.

No part of this book may be reproduced in any form, by photocopying or by any electronic or mechanical means, including information storage or retrieval systems, without permission in writing from both the copyright owner and publisher of this book.

Scripture quotations marked as (NIV) are taken from *THE HOLY BIBLE, NEW INTERNATIONAL VERSION®, NIV® Copyright © 1973, 1978, 1984, 2010 by Biblica, Inc.™* Used by permission. All rights reserved worldwide.

Scripture quotations marked as (NKJV) are taken from the *New King James Version. Copyright © 1982 by Thomas Nelson, Inc.* Used by permission. All rights reserved.

Scripture quotations marked (WUEST) are taken from *The New Testament: An Expanded Translation (WET) by Kenneth S. Wuest. Copyright © 2000-2010 Wm. B. Eerdmans Publishing Company.* All rights reserved.

Scripture quotations marked (ESV) are taken from *The Holy Bible (English Standard Version®) by Crossway.* All rights reserved.

Scripture quotations marked (AMP) are taken from the *Amplified® Bible, Copyright © 1954, 1958, 1962, 1964, 1965, 1987 by The Lockman Foundation.* Used by permission. www.lockman.org

Scripture quotations marked (NLT) are taken from the *Holy Bible, New Living Translation copyright © 1996, 2004, 2007 by Tyndale House Foundation.* Used by permission of Tyndale House Publishers, Inc., Carol Stream, Illinois 60188. All rights reserved.

Scripture quotations marked (TCNT) are taken from the *Twentieth Century New Testament* Published in 1904.

A special thanks to:

Jan Boshoff – Editing & Proofreading

Lisa Ackerman – Cover design & Artwork

Dan Bowen, Heather Gill & Donna Isenor – Transcriptions

— www.TheLivingGraceProject.com —

Printed in Hong Kong

For more grace resources please visit:
www.NewNaturePublications.com

Contents

Introduction

So you've been established on the foundation of God's grace and wondering what's next? Now it's time to learn how to apply all those living truths into the supernatural lifestyle of grace! The purpose of this book is to help you now connect a theology of grace to a life of grace.

This book will help you catch the new wave of grace that God is releasing upon the earth today causing you to demonstrate, to the world, just how good the Good News of Jesus really is! The first wave was a grace "revolution". This second wave is a grace "application". And it comes now on a secure identity in Christ, pure New Covenant motives, and the love of God that is unstoppable!

Living Grace both reinforces the foundation of grace and builds masterfully upon it. It would be ambitious to think we could cover every aspect in this book and therefore it is simply the first volume of many more to come!

Living Grace is a synergetic combination of thirteen great men of God, well established in the Gospel of Grace, who have come together to show you how the grace of God both gives life, and is the only way of life! Each chapter contains distilled wisdom of glorious truth that has been stripped of naïve idealism, tested by the fires of adversity and trial, and proven fruitful and effectual. This book is not just talk, it's stuff that works! It doesn't come with ideals but with impartations of life!

With a combined ministry experience of over 230 years, having seen hundreds of thousands of souls saved, countless healings of all kinds, incredible signs and wonders, supernatural joy and freedom coming to entire communities, orphans, widows and the poor being cared for and loved, and the Gospel being preached to literally tens of millions of people worldwide – you will now be equipped with invaluable life lessons on how grace supernaturally empowers you to fulfill the calling that is on your life! And the best thing about it is that it's ridiculously simple and profoundly uncomplicated!

This is a message the entire world needs to hear, and that is why it cannot stop at just the English language. We are excited to announce that, together with New Nature Publications, the authors of *Living Grace* have decided to dedicate 100% of the profits from this book to translating and distributing it into every language of the world. All profits will go to this until the book is literally reaching every country on the planet! This is called "The Living Grace Project".

In buying this book you are partnering in this project with the authors and New Nature Publications by contributing to the Gospel reaching every people group on earth! Ambitious? Yes! But what an opportunity for people to see living grace in action!

(Please note that while all the authors have the same strong foundation of grace, they may not necessarily agree on every aspect and out-working of grace held by each author. We have no problem with this. In fact, it demonstrates true grace, in that it's possible to hold differing views and yet still walk in love and honor with each other in a united front that has great impact in this world. Grace is not an argument to be won, it's a person to be encountered – Jesus Christ. The more we encounter Him, the more we walk in His love and truth, and unity with one another.)

We pray this book blesses your socks off!

Join the buzz at:

— www.TheLivingGraceProject.com —

About the Authors

Benjamin Dunn and his wife, Stephanie, have spent the last 8 years traveling across America and the far corners of the world sharing their unique sound and loving the poor along the way. Their ministry, missions, message and band are about breathing fresh, new life into peoples' ideals about worship, music, creativity and ultimately about God and His infinite love. They are all about the discovery of the incomprehensible grace of God and its eruption from our hearts into song, art, discussion, theology and life. They are currently based in the United States.

— www.joyrevolution.com —

Ryan Rufus is a full time pastor at City Church International, and founder of New Nature Publications. He has a powerful teaching gift with profound insights into the Gospel of Grace. He is the author of three great books, *Extra Virgin Grace*, *Sanctification by Grace* and *Do Christians Still Have a Sinful Nature?*. He lives in Hong Kong with his wife, Kylie, and are the proud parents of Renae, Chloe, Kimberly and Asher.

— www.ccihk.com —

— www.ryanrufus.com —

Arthur Meintjes is a Bible teacher and conference speaker, and travels the world teaching the Good News of God's unconditional love, goodness and mercy to restore mankind. He is an adjunct lecturer at Andrew Wommack's Charis Bible College in Colorado Springs, and is also a frequent guest speaker at several other CBC campuses in the USA and the United Kingdom. Arthur is the author of *Knowing and Experiencing God* and co-author with his wife, Cathy, of *Grace and Faith Thoughts.* They have three children and currently reside in Colorado, USA.

— www.kingdomlifeministry.com —

Rob Rufus and his wife, Glenda, have been leading successful churches for over 30 years. They currently lead City Church International in Hong Kong. Rob is a highly sought after teacher who travels extensively throughout the world, bringing a profound revelation of the Gospel of Grace, along with demonstrations of God's power. His desire is to see people, churches and nations liberated with the transforming power of God's grace.

— www.ccihk.com —

Fini de Gersigny has been in ministry since his early twenties. He and his wife, Isi, ministered with Rob Rufus in their early church years in South Africa, and these days in Sydney, Australia, where they planted Jubilee Church in 1997. Jubilee has gained a reputation of being a church founded in grace and moving in the Holy Spirit. Many leaders and believers from around the nation visit their services and conferences to be equipped in the realms of

prophetic worship and supernatural ministry. Fini and Isi have 6 wonderful children and live in Sydney, Australia.

— www.jubilee.org.au —

Joshua Mills is an anointed minister of the Gospel, a recording artist, keynote conference speaker and author. He worships and preaches by standing within the cloud and ministering directly from the glory unto the people. Wherever he goes, the Lord confirms His Word with miraculous signs and wonders that testify of Jesus Christ. Traveling all over North America and around the world, he has been creating a realm of glory wherever he goes, with a clear message that "*praise changes the atmosphere*". Along with his wife, Janet Angela, he ministers to millions around the globe through radio, television, and online webcasts. They currently reside in Vancouver, Canada, along with their children, Lincoln and Liberty.

— www.newwineinternational.org —

Cornel Marais is founder of Charisma Ministries and author of the book *So You Think Your Mind Is Renewed?* and the manual *Administering The Children's Bread: The Basics of Healing Under the New Covenant* which has been translated into 5 different languages. Cornel and his wife, Rensia, are originally from South Africa, but currently live in Hong Kong. Cornel has been traveling, writing, preaching and speaking internationally in churches and conferences in South Africa, Asia, New Zealand and America for the last 10 years.

— www.charismaministries.org —

Andrew Wommack has traveled America and the world teaching the truth of the Gospel for over four decades. His profound revelation of the Word of God is taught with clarity and simplicity, emphasizing God's unconditional love and the balance between grace and faith. He reaches millions of people through the daily Gospel Truth radio and television programs, broadcast both domestically and internationally. He is the founder of Charis Bible College, Colorado (in 1994) and has since established numerous CBC extension schools across America and the world. Andrew has also produced a library full of teaching materials available in print, audio, and visual formats. He and his wife, Jamie, live in Colorado Springs, USA.

— www.awmi.net —

Chad M. Mansbridge is the Lead Pastor at Bayside Church International, Victor Harbor, South Australia, which he, and his wife, Jaye, planted in 2002. Chad is the author of a powerful book called *He Qualifies You!*. He has an unshakable desire to see people walk in an authentic and unhindered relationship with their Maker, and through that experience, be empowered to represent Him well before others.

— www.baysidechurch.org.au —

— www.hequalifiesyou.com —

John Crowder and his wife, Lily, have a passion to spread the supernatural Gospel of Jesus Christ in its exuberant love and joy. The Crowders are founders of Sons of Thunder Ministries and Publications, and minister all over the world. Along with thousands of articles, John has also authored

four books: *The New Mystics*, *The Ecstasy of Loving God*, *Seven Spirits Burning*, and *Mystical Union*. John and Lily work to foster a creative new movement of ecstatic believers who are enthralled by the finished work of Christ, and who demonstrate miraculous lifestyles and supernatural joy. John has a vision to equip a supernatural generation to walk in the glory – clearly communicating the finished work of the Cross and operating in signs, wonders, and the divine intimacy needed for the last-day harvest. Sons of Thunder plants churches, children's homes for orphans, and hosts evangelism campaigns, conferences, and schools across the globe. Creative miracles and unusual signs and wonders mark John's ministry. He and his wife have four children and currently live in Santa Cruz, USA.

— www.thenewmystics.com —

Paul Hernandez is the Executive Director of F.R.E.E. Mission Philippines and Senior Pastor of Evangelical F.R.E.E. Church. He is involved in planting and building churches across the Philippines, and regularly hosts large leadership conferences to help establish people and churches in the Gospel of Grace. He is married to his lovely wife, Rucelle, and is the proud father of Phoebe, Johann and David.

— www.freemissionphils.com —

— www.ptrpaul.blogspot.com —

Wayne Duncan pastors a church with the woman of his dreams, Jennifer, in Port Edward, South Africa. Wayne is the author of *A Matter of Life and Death*, a book about how to read the Bible through the New Covenant lenses of grace. He has a passion to see all come in to a deeper revelation of who they are in Christ, and how to walk in that inheritance. He preaches in many churches every year, showing how to receive and walk in all that Christ has freely made available through His finished work.

— duncansportedward@telkomsa.net —

Lucas Miles is a sought after writer, speaker, church consultant, and pastor, having traveled to over 16 countries to minister the message of God's goodness with people all around the world. He is President of the Oasis Network For Churches, a radical grace based church planting and resourcing organization. He is also the senior pastor of Oasis Granger, which he and his wife, Krissy, planted in 2004. Lucas is the founder of the North American Grace Association and is one of the keynote speakers of the yearly North American Grace Conference. He commonly shares on television, in churches, universities, and conferences throughout the United States and abroad. He and his wife currently live in Indianapolis, USA.

— www.oasnet.org —

— www.northamericangraceassociation.com —

CHAPTER 1

Union

by Benjamin Dunn

Outrageous Oneness

Do you want to know what is so outrageously good about the Gospel?

It is not the hope of one day becoming nearer to God.

It is not the hope of one day becoming free from sin.

It is not the hope of heaven to come.

No, none of these can even remotely compare to the ludicrousness of the Gospel.

What truly makes the Gospel so ridiculously good, is the shocking announcement that believers are now, by faith, at once, and for all time, in union with Christ!

It is the absurd proclamation that our nearness to God has already been completed and perfected.

It is the innocent and audacious statement that we are already free from sin by having shared in Christ's death.

It is the brash declaration that all of Heaven has been given to us already—in Christ.

You may say, "This is outrageous!"

And I would answer, "I know, but it is the Gospel!"

And to tell you the truth, this is what makes my heart beat nearly out of my chest with excitement!

"...We are those who have become permanently united with Him."

- Romans 6:6 (Wuest Translation)

Does this shock you also?

I sure hope so, because this is the kind of truth that shocks corpses out of their graves!

Shock therapy is the Gospel's M.O.

You may ask, "But how are such things possible in this life?"

And I would say, "They aren't, but thank God impossibilities have never been an issue with Him!"

What I mean, is that they are perfectly impossible in our own strength and within our own willpower.

But that's just it – we are no longer our own.

We are not living by our willpower; we are living by His. We are not living by our abilities; we are living by His.

We have been joined to Christ in a vital and living union, in that He made Himself one with our curse and one with our fallenness, and ended them in His death.

It is a religious fantasy to think that we had, or have, anything at all to do with this union other than receiving it as a gift, and enjoying its goodness.

We must realize that our religious 'Towers of Babel' could not have reached even a fraction of the way to Heaven. God simply does not speak the language of self-effort. To Him it is all nonsense and noise.

Is the sacrifice of the Lamb enough to secure such an outlandish union?

Is it truly possible that this is the worth of Christ's sacrifice?

Let your futile efforts be swallowed up into Christ's infinite effort, and join the song of the heavens in singing, "*Yes, worthy is the slain Lamb!*" (Revelation 5:12)

Let your heart be overwhelmed by this outrageous oneness!

Union in the Incarnation

We have to see that the reality of the Gospel is not that God became *one of us*, but that *He became us*!

He was not Crucified *for my sin*, but *as my sin.*

This is the outrageous claim of the Gospel – that humanity's fallenness was consumed in Christ, and crucified upon the tree of Calvary.

It is as Romans 5 says: Just as all were made sinners through first Adam, even more are all made righteous through the last Adam (Christ).

This is the scandalous grace of God within the incarnation of Christ. God made Christ to actually become our sin. He actually became our evil, so that with His servant body He could carry our sin away!

Imagine this, better yet, let this reality hit you:

> "The Eternal Being, who knows everything and who created the whole universe, became not only a man, but (before that) a baby, and before that a fetus inside of a woman's body."
>
> - C.S. Lewis, Mere Christianity

If you want to get the hang of it, think of how you would like to become a slug.

The fathomless, immeasurable, independent, uncreated God, because of His great love for us, became man and swallowed our evil.

In fact, He came in the most helpless and dependent form that man can be in – an infant!

The Uncreated – became the created.

The Independent – became dependent.

The Eternal – became subject to time.

He who knew nothing of sin, nothing of unrighteousness, who knew nothing but good – became sin for us!

This is love!

This is the Gospel!

> "In the Incarnation, God the Son takes the body and human soul of Jesus, and, through that, the whole environment of nature, all the creaturely predicament, into His own being."
>
> - C.S. Lewis, Letters to Malcolm

So that "He came down from Heaven" can almost be transposed into "Heaven drew Earth up into it," and locality, limitation, sleep, sweat, footsore, weariness, frustration, pain, doubt, and death, are from before all worlds, known by God from within.

The Pure Light walks the earth, darkness, received into the heart of deity, is there swallowed up. Where, except in uncreated light, can darkness be drowned?"

The question is then: Have you seen your darkness swallowed in the uncreated light of Christ?

Have you seen your separation from God swallowed into Christ's crucified body on the Cross?

This is the reason He came, the reason He was incarnated – to take away forever our sinfulness and separation.

God prepared for Christ a body to offer. (Hebrews 10:5)

Christ became one with humanity for that very purpose – to remove our separation and become united to us!

And truly, what separated us from God was the separation itself, this being our independent and demanded self-existence apart from all that He is.

In fact, sin isn't what causes separation – it is separation that causes sin. When we were severed from God in our pre-Christ self-existence, sin was our world, we breathed its air and followed its impulses.

None of us had to try hard to sin, it was just our natural habitat. This was because we were apart from God, disconnected from real life.

All righteousness, life and goodness are found in Him; even more still, outside of Him there is not one single ounce of it to be found.

The only existence that is found outside of Christ is a sinful one.

What else do we expect to find?

Independence = Sin

Dependence = Perfection

Our perfection is totally dependent upon our union with the Perfect One. Union with Christ is our design, and man is perfect when he is perfectly united with Christ.

Humanity was created to be dependent upon God. We were never made to be anything on our own. This is exemplified in many scriptures where man is described as a branch (dependent upon the vine), as clay (dependent upon the potter), and as vessels (dependent upon the treasure within it).

If we look at all living things on Earth, we see that the dominant principle upon which all life hangs, is dependence.

Man is dependent on the animals and crops for food, the animals are dependent upon the fruit of the trees, and the trees are dependent upon water, soil, minerals, and light.

At the end of this chain of dependence we must all see that it is God Himself that upholds all things, and it is through Him that all things exist.

We have to realize that our whole existence is dependent upon Him alone!

> "Every man, woman, and child all over the world is feeling and breathing at this moment only because of God."
>
> - C.S. Lewis

Jesus said, "Without me you can do nothing!"

That really means nothing!

It is His breath that fills your lungs at this very moment. Go ahead, breathe – just like Adam, you too are dependent upon God to breathe into your nostrils.

It is He who animates your heart, giving it life and vitality, planning every single beat within your chest.

This is what Christ has done!

Rejoice that you are dependent, it is the sign of salvation!

Rejoice that Christ has united you to Himself and removed once and for all the whole of the sinfulness of mankind!

You may ask, "How can one bear the sin of all?"

This is the miracle of the incarnation!

This is why God became man!

C.S. Lewis writes:

> "There was a time when every man was a part of his mother, and (earlier still) part of his father as well, and when they were part of his grandparents. If you could see humanity spread out in time, as God sees it, it would not look like a lot of separate things dotted about. It would like one single growing thing—rather like a very complicated tree. Every individual would appear connected with every other."

The whole of humanity's darkness and evil was consumed in the body of Christ, crucified and buried forever.

Shouldn't we celebrate?

Do you see the scandalous love of God?

He did not wait for us to become one with Him. In Christ, God became one with humanity.

In the Incarnation, it is like God is saying to us,

> "I know that you will not, and simply cannot, come to me—so in my great love for you I will come to you! I will show you this infinite and unmatched love in that I will not ask you to rid yourself of your evil, for you are more filthy than you think and you cannot scrub the

stains from your heart, but I will rid it for you, and I will give you a new heart. I will not ask for your sweat and blood in this operation, for your wretchedness has infected and contaminated every single one of your cells, but I will shed My sweat and My blood for you! For, this impossible task of turning you to Myself can only be met by Me, who alone conquers the impossible, sustains the universe, creates everything out of nothing and knows all the hairs upon your head without counting.

This is My Gift to you—it is Myself."

Do you see His ridiculous grace? Jesus didn't just take our curse – He became our curse!

> "For, He became 'The Accursed' for our sakes."
>
> - Galatians 3:13 (A.S. Way Translation)

He didn't just pay for my sin – He became my sinfulness!

Paul writes:

> "Christ was innocent of sin, and yet for our sake God made Him one with the sinfulness of man."
>
> - 2 Corinthians 5:21 (New English Bible)

Here is that same verse from one of my favorite translations; St. Paul from the Trenches:

> "For this is the reconciliation—that even the sinful part of man… …the erroneous side of life was corrected by the eternal Christ, who Himself knew no sin, and yet presented in His own person… the death of sin, as though He had been sin Himself."
>
> - 2 Corinthians 5:21 (St. Paul from the Trenches)

Wow!

We have to see that in the Crucifixion of Christ, all that separated us from Him also died.

Absolutely everything!

Our sinfulness, our curses, our fear and hatred of God—all died in the death of Christ.

Here is another heart-exploding treasure from the St. Paul from the Trenches Translation:

> "I see in His one death, the death of all of us already accomplished…
> the death, that is to say, of all that separates us from God."
>
> - 2 Corinthians 5:14 (St. Paul from the Trenches)

Do you see also, in the death of Christ, the death of all that separated you from God?

When we see salvation from these eyes of faith and unmoved trust in the sacrifice of Christ, our own futile and infantile efforts at union and closeness to God become eclipsed by union's reality.

We simply find that it's already done, and the pleasure of it overtakes us!

This ends the search for nearness, for in this union with Christ we find God ever present – filling the deepest parts of our hearts.

This ends the pursuit for holiness, for in this union we find that we are eternally connected to Him who is our holiness.

What can be added to the sacrifice of the perfect Lamb of God?

What can we fulfill that He did not already perfect?

Oh my friends, you will stumble upon so much pleasure when you can boldly and blissfully answer—*Absolutely nothing!*

Siamese Union

In the epistles of Paul, we find this union with Christ everywhere, and from this perspective alone, he writes his letters.

This was no figurative or symbolic union; this union was real in the Apostle Paul's whole existence. It was his every breath. This drink of union had satiated Paul to the fullest and had become his daily bread and wine, and the essence of his teaching.

This union with Christ must also be our daily bread and wine!

Just look, for example, at what Paul writes in Colossians – that *Christ is our life.* (Colossians 3:4)

> "It is not enough to have said that the life is shared with Christ. The Apostle declares that Christ is the life…
>
> …This is not to be toned down to mean that Christ is the possessor and giver of eternal life. Paul means quite literally what he says, that Christ Himself is the essence of the Christian life."
>
> - Wuest Word Studies

Christ has become the very blood flowing within our veins and the breath within our lungs. This union is genuine and living!

You may ask, "But where did this union take place?"

Paul declares in Romans that our union with Christ took place in His death! That is where it began, and that is where our separated, sinful, and fallen condition ended.

Yes, you read it right – it has ended!

This is His gift to us!

Shall we not open it?

One of the most potent, persuasive, and intoxicating words I have found that the Apostle Paul uses in the scriptures, to describe our union with Christ, is the Greek word or prefix *sun*.

It denotes an extremely close and intimate union. Strong's adds that it also includes completeness; this prefix is used in many places within the epistles of Paul.

It is used in Romans 6 when he speaks of us being "*planted together*" in Christ's death.

Allow me to bring out a few riches from my translation library:

> "We have become **one with Him** (as a graft becomes one with a tree-stock through an experience corresponding to His death…"
>
> - Romans 6:5 (Wade Translation)

> "We have been made, **fellow plants in the garden of His death.**"
>
> - Romans 6:5 (Cotton Patch Translation)

> "We have become **one with Him** by sharing His death."
>
> - Romans 6:5 (Weymouth Translation)

The Greek word that the Apostle Paul uses here is *sumphutos*. Its definition is mind blowing!

It means that we are "connate with Christ" (Strong's) or "born together and so sharing the same nature" (Thayer's Bible Definition). Which is to say that we have been fused together with Him.

> "It speaks of a living, vital union of two individuals growing up together. The word is used of the Siamese twins whose bodies were connected at one point, and whose blood flowed through two physical bodies as it does normally through one. Here the word speaks of that vital union of the believer and the Lord Jesus where God places him into Christ at the Cross."
>
> - Wuest Word Studies

This is a past and complete act, yet its results are ever abiding with us.

Reader, can you feel Him even now warming your heart with His eternal presence flowing inside of you? He is not far; He is under your skin!

You have been grafted into Him so to share His life. You have been planted into unbroken fellowship with God Himself.

I simply cannot see the lack in what He has done for us.

Let us stop wanting and start enjoying!

So you see, it is from the soil of His death that this union blossoms.

> "When the seed or plant is inserted in the ground, it derives from that ground all its nourishment, and all those juices by which it becomes developed; by which it increases in size, grows firm, strong, and vigorous; puts forth its leaves, blossoms, and fruit.
>
> The death of Jesus Christ is represented as the cause whence his fruitfulness, as the author of eternal salvation to mankind is derived; and genuine believers in him are represented as being planted in his death, and growing out of it; deriving their growth, vigor, firmness, beauty, and fruitfulness from it.

> In a word, it is by his death that Jesus Christ redeems a lost world; and it is from that vicarious death that believers derive that pardon and holiness which makes them so happy."
>
> - Adam Clarke Commentary on the Whole Bible

Let your heart blossom into happy praises and thankfulness that this union with Christ is perfect and complete. Simply trust in the infinite power of His death and your union with Him will become your reality.

> "Look at it thus: do you not comprehend that all of us, who passed by baptism into **union** with Messiah Jesus, were by baptism made sharers in His death?
>
> ...As Messiah was raised from the dead by means of the descent of His Father's glory, so we too who rose with Him, are to be **employed wholly** in the activities of the New Life...
>
> ...We have entered into **living union with Him**."
>
> - Romans 6:4-5 (A.S. Way Translation)

CHAPTER 2

Totally Forgiven, Totally United, Totally Filled

by Ryan Rufus

Here are three truths that will ruin you forever, in a good way that is! Once these are in your heart, your life will take on a persona of peace, security, stability and confidence like never before. You will live free from useless religious activities and find it easier to live in the sweet spot of a supernatural grace life

Totally Forgiven

> "When you were dead in your sins and in the uncircumcision of your sinful nature, God made you alive in Christ. **He forgave us all our sins"**
>
> - Colossians 2:13 (NIV)

Most Christians have no trouble believing that Jesus has forgiven them of all their *past* sins. Many, however, have great trouble believing that Jesus has already forgiven them of all their *future* sins as well. Because of this lack in revelation, they feel they have to continually confess and repent of their sins and be cleansed of them, and they feel far from God until they have done so. They get caught up in what the Bible calls "*dead works*" or "*faithless works*" because they do not have a revelation of total forgiveness.

The truth is, God doesn't forgive us our sins, He *forgave* us our sins! Forgiveness is past tense, not future tense. It is a completed work, not something we hope will happen one day, and is also not an ongoing process via installments. Our forgiveness is past tense, it happened 2000 years ago. When we came into Christ, we came into total and complete forgiveness of all the sins we have ever committed, and all the sins we will ever commit! The Cross looked ahead at every sin and dealt with it right there!

If the Cross only dealt with past sins, it would mean that only those who sinned before the crucifixion could be forgiven. Everyone born after

Jesus would not be able to receive forgiveness and would be stuck with their sin! Their only hope would be for Jesus to be crucified again.

Similarly, if Jesus' crucifixion didn't atone for your future sin, then every time you sin, He would have to be crucified again in order for those newly committed sins to be atoned for. This is clearly impossible as Christ can never die again! Nor is it necessary. The Bible is clear, He forgave us *all* our sins - past, present and future!

The reason many can't accept this, is because they still have an Old Covenant mindset of having to offer a sacrifice to pay for their sin. When you don't see how the "*once for all*" sacrifice of Christ has completely dealt with all sin, from the start of time to the end of time, then you'll feel you need to continually offer something to pay for your sin and get rid of the guilt. Look at how the book of Hebrews explains this.

> "[11] Day after day every priest stands and performs his religious duties; again and again he offers the same sacrifices, which can never take away sins. [12] But when this priest had offered for all time one sacrifice for sins, he sat down at the right hand of God, [13] and since that time he waits for his enemies to be made his footstool. [14] For by one sacrifice he has made perfect forever those who are being made holy."
>
> - Hebrews 10:11-14 (NIV)

Did you notice, in there, one of the most powerful verses in the entire Bible?

Here it is again, *"But when this Priest had offered for all time one sacrifice for sins."* This scripture is saying that Jesus offered one sacrifice for all sin, for all time! Not many sacrifices, but one sacrifice. Not some sins, but all sin. Not just time past, but for all time! That means past, present and future sin! All sin was included and completely dealt with!

I want to declare to you today that all of your future sins have already been forgiven, even before you have committed them!

Knowing this will seriously affect how you live your life and the relationship you enjoy with God. It will free you from a whole lot of lifeless rituals and release you into a new and living way of serving God and being fruitful.

> "How much more shall the blood of Christ, who through the eternal Spirit offered himself without spot to God, purge your conscience from dead works to serve the living God?"
>
> - Hebrews 9:14 (NIV)

Many Christians, when they sin, feel unrighteous, dirty and guilty. They feel they have let God down and that God is no longer pleased with them. Their guilt then drives them to try and deal with their sin. So they pray and confess their sin. They repent and promise God that they will never do it again. Do you know that there is no Scripture under the New Covenant that commands born-again believers to confess their sins, repent of them, or even ask God to now forgive them? I know this challenges our modern day sin conscious mindset and strikes fear into the hearts of some believers who think this will lead to a casting off of restraint. But to confess, repent and ask God for forgiveness of sins is a contradiction to the Gospel. Why? Because by *one* sacrifice He has dealt will *all* your sins for *all* time! And you need to go back and have a good look at all the scriptures that people use to try and get you confessing and repenting, in their proper context. You'll be surprised!

Under the New Covenant, we are not called to confess our sins, we are called to confess our righteousness in Jesus Christ!

Take your eyes off your sin and get your eyes onto Christ. The more you do that, the more you will overcome sin in your life!

We are not even called to ask for forgiveness if and when we sin now! I know this confounds the traditional ways in which we were discipled. You may have been taught in church that, as a Christian, after you sin, you have to confess your sin and ask for forgiveness. But let me ask you this, have you found where the Bible teaches that in the New Covenant? You shouldn't always believe everything we preachers tell you! You should always find out for yourself and then base your life on the truth of the Word of God, not just on what someone else says.

The desire to want to say sorry to God and to ask for forgiveness is the result of a conscience that is more aware of the Tree of the Knowledge of Good and Evil than a consciousness of the finished work of Christ. A conscience that wants to get rid of guilt by practicing these dead work rituals is a conscience that needs to be washed by the the blood of Jesus. You need to renew your conscience to grace.

Of course we'll feel guilt after sin. That's normal. Something would be seriously wrong if we didn't! But it's how we deal with that guilt that's important. Do we try to achieve righteousness and forgiveness, or do with rest in the finished work of Christ and confess our perfect righteousness and purity in Him?

This is the kind of confession I make if I mess up, "God, I'm sorry. I did not want to do that. That's not part of my new creation nature. But I am not going to get all morbid and introspective or sorrowful and guilty! You don't want that. You want me to lift up my head and stay in the spirit, and to thank You for Your free gift of righteousness and total forgiveness. I fix my eyes and consciousness on Jesus whose blood has washed away all my sin. Thank You that I am the righteousness of God in Christ Jesus. I believe it!"

God doesn't want guilt-ridden introspection that focuses on our sin. He wants us to continually focus on Him. For many years in my Christian life I would always feel like I needed to ask God for forgiveness when I sinned. In fact, I did always ask God, "God please forgive me. Please cleanse me." That was until I came into the revelation of *total* forgiveness! Once I came into the revelation of total forgiveness, do you know what started to happen? When I sinned and went to God to ask for forgiveness, I would hear the voice of the Father saying straight back to me, *"Ryan, I already have! I did it two thousand years ago at the Cross. And you know all those sins you are going to commit in the future? I have already forgiven those too!"*

Christians who are not secure in grace will immediately say, "Oh, come now Ryan, be careful! If you say this stuff, Christians are going to go wild and sin even more!" They say this as though having to ask God for forgiveness after they've sinned is a deterrent that stops believers from sinning. But let me ask this: Which has the most potential to stop you from sinning, knowing you are forgiven before you sin, or knowing you can get forgiveness after you sin? Neither! Christians will sin either way! Some people accuse grace as just a license to sin, and think that if we were a bit under the law then we wouldn't sin. They say this as though law is not a license to sin. Yet under the law if you sinned you could go and offer a sacrifice for that sin and you'd be forgiven.

I don't know about you, but I'm born-again! I don't want to sin. My new nature, God's nature, wants to live for God. It wants to serve God! It is not even a sacrifice! The desire and passion of my spirit is to live one hundred percent for God! And if I could live just by my reborn spirit – my new creation nature, then I would live absolutely perfect for God and in His perfect will. The problem is that our body and our mind get in the way, and are tempted by sin because they haven't been made perfect yet. My mind and my body may get tempted to sin, but the real me, my spirit, doesn't want to sin. Sin is foreign to my new nature. This is why the Bible says we must offer our bodies as living sacrifices and renew our minds. This simply means learning how to surrender our mind and our body to our spirit so that our spirit is in control and leads us. As we walk by our spirit, we will live out all the riches of God's nature that He put inside of our spirit at the point of salvation.

> "...and to put on the new self, created after the likeness of God in true righteousness and holiness."
>
> - Ephesians 4:24 (ESV)

Your new nature has been created after the nature of God in perfect righteousness and perfect holiness. The Bible says that God has put His law in our hearts (Hebrews 8 & 10). That's not talking about the Ten Commandments. Goodness gracious, if God did that it would just kill us! No, the law which God put on our hearts is His nature. It is His perfect nature.

No one has to say to God, "God, You shouldn't lie. You shouldn't steal. You shouldn't commit adultery." Why? Because it's not in His nature. His nature is perfect! God cannot sin. And when we live by our new nature, we live by His desires, His perfect and holy nature. This is when sin becomes easy to overcome! Now, let us continue with our original point.

As a New Covenant, born-again believer, to go and ask God for forgiveness after you have sinned, is in fact, a sin! It is the sin of unbelief. You don't believe in the finished work of the Cross, and therefore you are trying to achieve what you don't realize you already have: Total forgiveness of all sin from the start of your life to the end of your life.

Preaching total forgiveness is not giving people a license to sin. I don't personally know of any grace preachers that are preaching a license to sin, not one! However, if you do sin, (now brace yourself...) don't start asking God for forgiveness. Don't start confessing that sin and repenting of that

sin. Get your eyes on Jesus and keep your faith in Him! Keep walking in the spirit covenant, the grace covenant. Keep declaring your absolute forgiveness. Confess your righteousness and keep reminding yourself of the finished work of Christ!

"Father thank You that even this sin has been dealt with, and I am still perfectly righteous!"

Do you know that some Christians think that when you sin you become unholy until you have confessed, repented, been forgiven and cleansed of that sin? Do you know that is absolute deception? Other than Scripture being abundantly clear about that, there is another proof that your purity and your relationship with God is not broken by sin. It's called the ever-abiding presence of the Holy Spirit! If your sin made you unholy and unrighteous, then the Holy Spirit would have to leave you every time you sinned, until you received forgiveness and were "made holy" again. You would have to be re-baptized in the Holy Spirit. That is ridiculous! He never leaves! He is ever present! Why? Because you are ever righteous, ever holy, and eternally forgiven! Joy comes when we believe that!

The Gospel of Grace should make you happy because it is good news! It is always good news! If someone turns the good news into bad news, don't listen to them! They are not preaching the good news. It is always good and should always make you happy and produce supernatural joy, peace and freedom in you.

Totally United With Christ

"If we have been united with him like this in his death, we will certainly also be united with him in his resurrection."

- Romans 6:5 (NIV)

> "And God raised us up with Christ and seated us with him in the heavenly realms in Christ Jesus."
>
> - Ephesians 2:6 (NIV)

> "But he who unites himself with the Lord is one with him in spirit."
>
> - 1 Corinthians 6:17 (NIV)

This is one of the most profound revelations that you will ever have. Your spirit has been fully united with Christ. That means that you are united with Christ in His death, in His burial, in His resurrection, in His ascension and in being seated on the throne at the right hand of the Father.

Everything that happened to Jesus also happened to you. You receive the benefits of it all, yet without having to physically go through it. He hung on the Cross in our place. He took all our sins and sicknesses and the full weight of the judgment and wrath of God. Thank God we didn't have to face that judgment! Jesus faced that for us so we will never have to!

If God has already punished Christ for your sins, He cannot then punish you for those same sins! Some people preach as though God is going to punish you for your sins. Some will preach that God has made you sick because He is punishing you for your sins. If that were the case, then God is dishonoring the Cross. The Bible says that Jesus was punished for all of our sins. God will never ever punish you with sickness because of sin in your life.

Some of you reading this are sick and think it is God punishing you for your sin. You need to get free right now in Jesus Name! You need to challenge that lie that is from the pit of Hell and reject it. You have been forgiven of all your sin, therefore it is impossible that God has afflicted you because of sin. Challenge that lie and receive your healing right now!

You died with Christ, you were buried with Christ, and you were raised

to new life in Christ. You used to be dead to God, but then God raised you up in new creation life in Christ. The life of Christ is now your life. You were born again! All people are born naturally of water (flesh), but as a believer, you have been supernaturally born of the spirit by the Holy Spirit, who made you alive with Christ.

> "[4] But because of his great love for us, God, who is rich in mercy, [5] made us alive with Christ…."
>
> - Ephesians 2:4-5 (NIV)

Do you know where you are seated right now in the spiritual realms? On the throne with Christ! You are a co-heir with Christ and joined to Him. That is greater than any of us realize. That is so powerful and extremely profound. You are seated with Christ and reigning together with Christ!

Do you know that when you experienced the miracle of rebirth through faith in Christ, your spirit was united with Christ in His death, burial, resurrection, and glorification? Do you know that once that has happened to you, it can never be undone? Do you know what that means? It means that you can never lose your salvation! Why? Because Christ is your life. In order for you to lose your salvation, you would have to spiritually die again. But it is impossible for you to spiritually die, because you are united with Christ and His life is now your life. That is our eternal guarantee! He will *never* die again! He has an indestructible life. He is our High Priest in the order of Melchizedek, and He ever lives to intercede for us. And because we are united with Him, that means we can never die again! If you can never die again then you can never lose your salvation!

> "[24] But because Jesus lives forever, he has a permanent priesthood. [25] Therefore he is able to save completely those who come to God through him, because he always lives to intercede for them."
>
> - Hebrews 7:24-25 (NIV)

I have looked at many of the scriptures that seem to imply that you can lose your salvation, but when those scriptures are read in their proper context, they actually only reinforce the fact that you *can't* lose your salvation! People have taken those scriptures and used them to try and put illegitimate fear into Christians, to motivate them to live a certain way for God. But that's not true New Covenant motivation of faith, love, and hope in the Spirit. Rather, it's that Old Covenant manipulative motivation of blessings and curse. I don't resist sin because I'm scared of God's judgment or losing my salvation. I resist sin because I love God and His nature is inside of me. I don't serve God because I'm scared of what will happen if I don't, or because I want to get some blessing. I serve Him because my spirit has been awakened to Him and my spirit is full of His passion, love, and purpose.

Don't ever be manipulated to serve God. You don't need to be manipulated to serve God! Your spirit wants to serve God! It's been united with Christ. You have all of His life inside of you! If you are a leader you don't need to manipulate Christians into serving God with clever techniques. You don't need to make Christians fearful in order to motivate them to do things for God, or promise them special blessings. No! Teach them about what has happened inside of them. Show them their new nature and what God has done in their spirit and watch those Christians come alive. You won't be able to stop them from serving God!

Totally Filled

> "[9] For in Christ all the fullness of the Deity lives in bodily form, [10] and you have been given fullness in Christ"
>
> - Colossians 2:9-10 (NIV)

Christ is fully God, and you have been fully united with Christ. Therefore,

all of the fullness of God is in you now! All the riches of Heaven, and all of the perfection of Christ, lives inside of you right now! There is nothing of the old creation order that lives inside of your new creation spirit. There is no fallen sinful nature in there. There is no sin or unrighteousness. Your spirit has received full perfection, full holiness and the full nature of God. God is not trying to give you anything more of Himself in your spirit, He has already given you all of Himself! You already have it now! You're not in the process of receiving fullness, or living in hope of a future fullness, you *have* been given fullness in Christ!

Many people think that the fruit of the spirit is the fruit of the Holy Spirit. That's partly true. It's also the fruit of living under grace *and* the fruit of living by your reborn spirit! The fruit of the spirit is what is in your new nature. It's the result of your spirit being united with Christ. All of the fullness of God already lives inside of you. You have the fullness of God's love, joy, peace, patience, kindness, goodness, faithfulness, gentleness, self-control, and much more. The fruit of the Spirit is infinite! So when we walk in the Spirit by our reborn spirit, we manifest the fullness of God through our lives.

See, it's not about trying to walk in good behavior or getting all of our 'little disciples' behaving well and feeling proud as if we've done something for God, as though God would be proud of us if we cleaned only the outside of a bowl! No, it's all about walking in the Spirit. Good discipling is really about teaching people how to walk in the Spirit. The fruit of walking in the flesh results in bad behavior but the fruit of walking in the Spirit results in Heaven coming to Earth through us!

> "If we live in the Spirit, let us also walk in the Spirit."
>
> \- Galatians 5:25 (KJV)

The Bible reveals that when we are born again, we become alive in the spirit, or "*live in the Spirit*", and it also urges us to then walk in the spirit. But this is not automatic. It's still possible to walk in the flesh even after we've been born again. So walking in the spirit requires us to do something. So what does it mean to walk in the spirit and how do we do that?

There are three dimensions to walking in the spirit:

1. In the *Spirit* Covenant (the New Covenant)
2. By your reborn *spirit*
3. In fellowship with the Holy *Spirit*

How do you do this? By focusing on these three things, and by investing into these three areas. In other words, sow to the spirit and not the flesh. If you focus and live from the flesh, it will result in corruption and a downward spiral. If you focus and live from the spirit, it will result in a supernatural life, God's life, which is eternal life.

> "[8] For the one who sows to his own flesh will from the flesh reap corruption, but the one who sows to the Spirit will from the Spirit reap eternal life."
>
> - Galatians 6:8-9 (ESV)

Therefore, focus on the Spirit Covenant, not the Flesh Covenant. Be conscious of Christ and not of sin. If you sin, don't run back to the law and get under condemnation. Stay in the Spirit Covenant of grace and not the Flesh Covenant of law. Feed on the new way of the Spirit and detox from the old way of the letter.

Then also focus on your perfect, holy, and righteous reborn spirit. Become aware of who you really are, your true identity. You are a spirit that lives in a body and has a mind. But the real you is your spirit, which has been recreated in Christ's likeness. Confess that over yourself, instead of how dirty you think you are. Learn to make decisions from your spirit and not the feelings of your body or from the emotions or worldly wisdom of your mind. Learn how to become aware of your spirit. We're so aware of our mind and body. This is how most of the world lives: flesh conscious. But there is another realm that is far superior and more real – it's the spirit realm, the invisible realm, the eternal realm. Your spirit is infinitely bigger than your limited mind and body! Learn to awaken your spirit. Some of the ways to do this is to spend time praying in the spirit, worshiping God, soaking in His presence, and waiting on Him.

Then thirdly, walk in intimacy with the Holy Spirit daily. He is God inside of you! He will strengthen you, lead you, empower you, and help you to live from the spirit realm. You need regular powerful breakthrough prayer times with the Holy Spirit. Get to know Him as your closest friend. Talk to Him! He is your defender not your accuser! He's on your side and wants to help you, not condemn you. He wants to make Heaven, and all that is God's, manifestly real to you! (John 14 – 16, Hebrews 10:12-15, Romans 8, Acts.)

Unfortunately, much of the Church focuses on the weakness of people's bodies and the corruption of their minds far too often. The only result of this is condemnation and more sin. Rather, we should endeavor to activate an awareness of the spirit. As we do that, the spirit will take control over our body and mind, and we will overcome! One of the most effective and helpful things you can do is to teach believers how to walk in the spirit. You should sow into this and watch the harvest you reap!

A revelation of total forgiveness leads to confidence and a strong relationship with God. A revelation of being totally united with Christ leads to eternal security and true motivation to live for God. A revelation of having been totally filled with the fullness of Christ leads to a life of overflow and releasing rather than striving to get!

These are truths worth soaking in. Get them deeply established in your heart and look forward to some nice big tasty juicy fruit!

CHAPTER 3

Guilt Free Living

by Arthur Meintjes

Serving God with Pure Motives

For so many Christians, all they have ever known and believed about God and the Bible has been rooted in guilt, condemnation and fear. This has produced motives that are mostly inferior, rendering their Christian life difficult, unfulfilling and unproductive. This in turn, produced further emotions of indebtedness, obligation, and the fear of judgment and punishment. Ultimately, they have a mentality of performance and the desire for reward, which induces feelings of inferiority, a low sense of self-worth, depression, isolation and rejection.

The definition for "guilt" is very much the same as "judgment". It means; "*to be under sentence; condemnation, or brought to trial or justice*". The dictionary defines the word "guilt" as, "*A feeling of responsibility or remorse for some offense, crime or wrong, etc. whether real or imagined.*"

As Christians, our guilt goes even further, and is rooted in the belief of having offended a holy and righteous God. This issue of guilt is as old as man himself, it goes as far back as the first people on earth. Adam and Eve were the first to experience the problem of guilt after they ate the fruit of the tree that God specifically told them not to eat. Guilt has been part of man's psychological and emotional makeup ever since.

There is no emotion that is more destructive than the emotion of guilt, because at its root, guilt is the condition of being condemned and separated from a holy God and deserving of divine judgment and punishment. Constant guilt in a believer's life is not conducive to emotional well-being or victorious Christian living. Yet these are the very emotions many Christians live with all their lives. They believe it is normal to be weighed down with guilt, condemnation and fear, and many believe this kind of guilt to actually be a valid Christian emotion!

Statistics in the past have shown that people who are members of the Pentecostal, Charismatic, or Full-Gospel denominations, suffer from guilt and guilt related emotional disorders more than any other religious group in the world. Depression and related social disorders have reached epidemic proportions in the Western world. For the majority of believers, their emotions are so deeply rooted in guilt and condemnation, that it becomes almost impossible for them to respond correctly in their daily relationship with God.

Let me explain what I mean.

Most of us have loved ones that we enjoy spending time with. What would the correct emotional response be for any person who was not able to be with a loved one for a prolonged period of time? I believe that the correct emotional response would be a sense of longing and a desire to be with them and spend time with them. I spend a great deal of time away from my wife and family, and I know the deep longing for them when I am away. Sometimes all I want is just to be able to smell my wife, I long just to smell her perfume.

Well, we say that we love God and have a loving relationship with Him. What is the prevailing emotion most believers have when they fail to have personal time with God for a prolonged period? I would venture to say that for most, it would be guilt, condemnation, fear and a sense of failure. If we are really honest with ourselves, I'm sure we will admit that none of us can claim that we are entirely free from the influence of this kind of guilt in our Christian life. All of us, in one way or another, are either partially or wholly motivated by this hidden guilt.

Guilt Has its Roots in Self-Righteousness

The religious system that most of us have grown up with makes it almost impossible to live free from this kind of guilt. Most of what the Church believes about God and the Bible makes it almost impossible for people to live in the freedom and liberty that Jesus came to give. Many believers are totally entangled in religious legalistic self-righteousness, a toxic mixture of Old Testament law (or self-effort), and New Testament hope. It is in this religious system, deeply entrenched in the Church today, where all guilt has its root.

In Romans, Paul gives us a clear understanding about what happens to anyone who lives his or her Christian life under the law, or in works-righteousness and self-effort.

> "Now we know that whatever the law says, it says to those who are under the law, that every mouth may be stopped, and all the world may become guilty before God."
>
> - Romans 3:19 (NKJV)

Paul makes it very clear that the emotion of guilt is the direct result of living under the law, or in self-effort or works-righteousness. The implication is that guilt is one of the most self-righteous feelings or emotions that any believer can experience. When there is guilt in our lives, it is a strong indication that we are under law, that we are living in legalism and self-righteousness.

Now, I know that many Christians wonder how they will ever be motivated if they don't feel guilty, or if guilt does not play a significant part in their relationship with God. When you take away guilt motivation, many Christians are suddenly lost and don't know how to follow Jesus. In many circles today, guilt is seen as a means of overcoming the problems and the sins we have in our lives. In reality, whatever you still feel guilty about continues to have power over your life. It will bind you to the very thing you feel guilty about.

Guilt Free Living

Guilt free living is exactly what God wants for us as men and women of God. Freedom from guilt is at the very heart of God's plan for man, through the finished work of Jesus Christ.

> "[17] And He was handed the book of the prophet Isaiah. And when He had opened the book, He found the place where it was written:
> [18] 'The Spirit of the Lord is upon Me,
> Because He has anointed Me
> To preach the gospel to the poor;
> He has sent Me to heal the brokenhearted,
> To proclaim liberty to the captives
> And recovery of sight to the blind,
> To set at liberty those who are oppressed;
> [19] To proclaim the acceptable year of the Lord.'"
>
> - Luke 4:17-19 (NKJV)

In this passage of Scripture, Jesus quotes from Isaiah 61 and He proclaims the Jewish Year of Jubilee, when all debts are cancelled, all slaves are freed, and all property is returned to the original owners. Jesus makes it clear that not only is His ministry to set us free from sin, but also to cleanse us from a sense of indebtedness and guilt. See what the writer of Hebrews says about this:

"...When He had by offering Himself accomplished our cleansing of sins and riddance of guilt, He sat down at the right hand of the divine Majesty on high,"

- Hebrews 1:3 (AMP)

Jesus not only cleansed us of our sins, but also rid us of the guilt that came with the sin. There are multitudes of reasons why people live with the crippling effect of guilt in their lives. Some live with false guilt: This is the guilt that we put on each other in order to manipulate one another. Some live with real guilt: This is the guilt that haunts us because of the times in our lives when we have violated our conscience through things we have seen, or things that we have allowed ourselves to do. And then some people live with tremendous shame because of abusive relationships, or because of sexual abuse. I want to tell you today, that no matter what the source of your guilt is, God's will is for you to live guilt free.

Guilt of the Past

Some of the greatest sources of guilt, condemnation, and emotional distress in our lives, are the failures, mistakes, sins, indiscretions, and weaknesses of the past. For many, their future progress and happiness has been postponed or interrupted because of the guilt of the past. This does not need to be the case at all. In Jesus Christ, your future does not have to be determined by your past. According to the New Covenant truth of the finished work of the Cross, our whole future is determined by and through the life and the work of someone else, namely Jesus Christ of Nazareth. After all, the Gospel of Jesus Christ is not about your past, it is about your future.

"For if a man is in Christ he becomes a new person altogether – the past is finished and gone, everything has become fresh and new.

> ...God was in Christ personally reconciling the World to Himself – not counting their sins against them – and has commissioned us with the message of reconciliation."
>
> - 2 Corinthians 5:17-21 (J.B. Phillips Translation)

All your past – good or bad – is finished, gone. All your sin, all your failures, indiscretions and guilt of the past, is gone.

Behold the Lamb of God

Under the Old Covenant, when a man sinned, he could have his sins taken care of by taking a lamb to be sacrificed at the temple. The priest, representing God, would examine and scrutinize the lamb to find out if there was anything wrong with it. He would never examine or scrutinize the sinner, only the sacrifice. When the lamb had been examined and the priest was satisfied that it was spotless and pure, it would be sacrificed in place of the sinner, to pay for the sin of the man who was guilty. He would go free with a clear conscience before God.

In the Gospel of John, Jesus is referred to as the Lamb of God.

> "The next day John saw Jesus coming to him and said, 'Look! There is the Lamb of God, Who takes away the sin of the world!"
>
> - John 1:29 (AMP)

In the Luke 23, we find Pilate and Herod, the highest authorities of the day, examining Jesus, the Lamb of God. In verse 22, Pilate declares Jesus to be spotless, without a cause for death in Him.

"Then he said to them the third time, 'Why, what evil has He done? I have found no reason for death in Him. I will therefore chastise Him and let Him go.'"

- LUKE 23:22 (KJV)

Even so, Jesus is executed in place of the man who was put in prison for sedition and murder, giving us a wonderful picture of the great exchange. Because of Jesus, the Lamb of God, we can now live our lives free from sin and the penalty of that sin, knowing that sin is no longer an issue between us and God, living free from guilt, condemnation, and fear. Jesus truly is the Lamb of God who takes away the sin of the world!

The problem that we have in the heart of so many believers today, is that we see and even agree with John the Baptist, that Jesus is the Lamb of God who takes away the sin of the world. But in practice, we do not live our lives according to this truth. When we live with a guilty, evil conscience toward God, it means that we do not acknowledge Jesus Christ's sacrifice of propitiation!

The question that we need to ask ourselves is this: Did Jesus take away the sin of the world in and through His sacrifice of propitiation, or not?

The answer to this question is made clear to us through the many writings of Paul and John, and also the writer of Hebrews. So let us now look at some of these scriptures:

"[1] My little children, I write you these things so that you may not violate God's law and sin. But if anyone should sin, we have an Advocate (One Who will intercede for us) with the Father – [it is] Jesus Christ [the all] righteous [upright, just, Who conforms to the Father's will in every purpose, thought, and action].[2] And He [that same Jesus Himself] is

> the propitiation (the atoning sacrifice) for our sins, and not for ours alone but also for [the sins of] the whole world."
>
> - 1 John 2:1-2 (AMP)

The word *"propitiation"* used here, literally means, "The satisfying of the perfect justice of a holy and righteous God." Propitiation makes it possible for God to show complete mercy, without compromising the righteousness of His justice. So John writes that Jesus Himself is the propitiation (satisfying the perfect justice of a holy and righteous God) for our sin, and not just for our sin, but the sin of the whole world. According to John, Jesus took away the sin of the whole world!

Next, John proclaims the extent of God's love and writes:

> "9 In this the love of God was made manifest (displayed) where we are concerned: in that God sent His Son, the only begotten or unique [Son], into the world so that we might live through Him. 10 In this is love: not that we loved God, but that He loved us and sent His Son to be the propitiation (the atoning sacrifice) for our sins.
>
> - 1 John 4:9-10 (AMP)

Again, John uses this word *"propitiation"*, declaring the fact that the sacrifice of Jesus Christ has taken care of the sin problem between man and God.

> "Since all have sinned and are falling short of the honor and glory which God bestows and receives."
>
> - Romans 3:23 (AMP)

Unfortunately, most of the time people only read this verse and stop, leaving out the next couple of verses, leaving us without any hope. Paul uses this statement in verse 23 as a contrast to highlight the next two verses. Therefore, these verses need to be read and interpreted together.

"[24] [All] are justified and made upright and in right standing with God, freely and gratuitously by His grace (His unmerited favor and mercy), through the redemption which is [provided] in Christ Jesus, [25] Whom God put forward [before the eyes of all] as a mercy seat and propitiation by His blood [the cleansing and life-giving sacrifice of atonement and reconciliation, to be received] through faith. This was to show God's righteousness, because in His divine forbearance He had passed over and ignored former sins without punishment."

- Romans 3:24-25 (AMP)

Notice that the Amplified Bible helps us to see that we cannot just quote or use verse 23 by itself, because verse 24 also starts with the word "*All*". In verse 23, "*All have sinned*", but in verse 24, "*All are justified*" through the redemption that is in Christ Jesus. Then in verse 25 Paul tells us how God did this. By Jesus Christ's sacrifice of propitiation, passing over and ignoring former sin without punishment.

The Eternal Forgiveness of All Our Sin

When Jesus died on the Cross and was raised from the dead, He became the complete sacrifice for our sin once and for all. Satisfying the justice of a holy and righteous God for all eternity!

The writer of Hebrews says it like this:

"[24] For Christ (the Messiah) has not entered into a sanctuary made with [human] hands, only a copy and pattern and type of the true one, but [He has entered] into heaven itself, now to appear in the [very] presence of God on our behalf. [25] Nor did He [enter into the heavenly sanctuary to] offer Himself regularly again and again, as the high priest enters the [Holy of] Holies every year with blood not his own. [26]

> For then would He often have had to suffer [over and over again] since the foundation of the world? But as it now is, He has once for all at the consummation and close of the ages appeared to put away and abolish sin by His sacrifice [of Himself]"
>
> - HEBREWS 9: 24-28 (AMP)

Notice what the writer says in verse 26, *"But as it now is..."*. What he is saying is that this is how it is now, like it or not! This is how things are now because of the finished work of Jesus on the Cross! He has appeared to put away and abolish sin by His sacrifice, once, for all people, for all time, providing total forgiveness and pardon for all humanity's offenses against a holy God!

The writer goes on.

> "[27] And just as it is appointed for [all] men once to die, and after that the [certain] judgment, [28] Even so it is that Christ, having been offered to take upon Himself and bear as a burden the sins of many once and once for all, will appear a second time, not to carry any burden of sin **nor to deal with sin**, but to bring to full salvation those who are [eagerly, constantly, and patiently] waiting for and expecting Him."
>
> – HEBREWS 9:27-28 (AMP)

Here he makes it clear that this issue of sin is dealt with so completely and utterly, that even though Jesus will come again a second time, He will never have to deal with this matter again! It is done, and will never be an issue between man and God again.

Jesus fully provided forgiveness and pardon before a holy and perfect God! Leaving us the liberty to live free from guilt, condemnation, shame, and fear! In the kingdom of His Son, there is complete liberty to live free from guilt, condemnation, or fear of death through punishment, and the judgment of God for sin.

No More Consciousness of Sin!

The problem that many of us still have, is that we have been taught to believe that we should still feel guilty even after we have trusted Jesus to pay for our sin. One of the most awesome powers of the finished work of Jesus Christ, is that at the Cross, God's intent was not only to cleanse us of all our sin, but also to cleanse our consciences of all guilt.

In Hebrews 10, the writer continues by giving us some insight into what the results will be if we believe and start living according to the truth of the eternal forgiveness of all our sin.

1. Perfect

> "For since the Law has merely a rude outline (foreshadowing) of the good things to come – instead of fully expressing those things – it can never by offering the same sacrifices continually year after year make perfect those who approach [its altars]."
>
> -Hebrews 10:1 (AMP)

This word "*perfect*" used here is not about being made perfect in our moral behavior, but is about being made perfect in the sense of wholeness, soundness and peace! "Completeness", as in being made completely and perfectly innocent!

2. No Consciousness of Sin

> "For if it were otherwise, would [these sacrifices] not have stopped being offered? Since the worshipers had once for all been cleansed, they would no longer have any guilt or consciousness of sin."
>
> - Hebrews 10:2 (AMP)

The writer sets a premise here for what he is going to explain later! He clearly states that if there were a sacrifice that had the ability to take care of sin, and make a man completely and perfectly innocent, there would no longer be any guilt or consciousness of sin! That is as plain and clear as you will ever get.

3. The Blood of Bulls and Goats

> "Because the blood of bulls and goats is powerless to take sins away."
>
> - Hebrews 10:4 (AMP)

It is clear that the Old Testament system of law and sacrifices could not cleanse us of our sin, but instead gave us a consciousness of sin so we cannot live guilt free!

4. A Single Sacrifice for Sin Completely Cleansed and Perfected!

> "[12] Whereas this One [Christ], after He had offered a single sacrifice for our sins [that shall avail] for all time, sat down at the right hand of God. [13]. For by a single offering He has forever completely cleansed and perfected those who are consecrated and made holy."
>
> - Hebrews 10:12-14 (AMP)

The next ten verses make his case for the fact that there is now a sacrifice that has taken care of sin, once and for all eternity, and that by this single sacrifice God has cleansed and perfected every believer (made every believer completely and perfectly innocent)!

If that is true (and it is), then according to verse 2, it is also true that every believer today should no longer have any guilt or consciousness of sin!

5. God Has No Remembrance of Our Sin!

> "[17] He then goes on to say, And their sins and their lawbreaking I will remember no more. [18] Now where there is absolute remission (forgiveness and cancellation of the penalty) of these [sins and lawbreaking], there is no longer any offering made to atone for sin."
>
> - Hebrews 10:17-18 (AMP)

The reason we should have no more consciousness of sin today, is because according to Paul, God has no more remembrance of sin today. Because of the sacrifice of Jesus, we have absolute forgiveness and cancellation of the penalty for sin! The blood of Jesus also assures us that we need never make any other sacrifice to atone for our sin and lawbreaking! *No penance, no offerings, no vows or indulgences, no consecrations!*

6. Purified Conscience

> "[22] Let us all come forward and draw near with true (honest and sincere) hearts in unqualified assurance and absolute conviction engendered by faith (by that leaning of the entire human personality on God in absolute trust and confidence in His power, wisdom, and goodness), having our hearts sprinkled and purified from a guilty (evil) conscience and our bodies cleansed with pure water."
>
> - Hebrews 10:22 (AMP)

The blood of Jesus not only cleansed us of all our sin, but also if we believe and trust in the power and virtue of the blood of Jesus, it will cleanse and rid us of a guilty conscience.

The Guarantee

There is a guarantee that accompanies this wonderful truth of the finished work of Jesus on the Cross.

> "[8] And he guarantees right up to the end that you will be counted free from all sin and guilt on that day when he returns. [9] God will surely do this for you, for he always does just what he says, and he is the one who invited you into this wonderful friendship with his Son, even Christ our Lord."
>
> - 1 Corinthians 1:8-9 (Living Bible)

Note that this scripture says that God guarantees you and I, that because of the finished work of Jesus on the Cross two thousand years ago, we will be counted free from all sin and all guilt on that day when He returns.

What an absolutely wonderful promise this is to us today. God wants you and I to live our lives free from sin and from guilt. Guilt free living is God's best for His people. Will you accept His guarantee for your life today and start living guilt free?

Chapter 4

The Grace-Hating Spirit

by Rob Rufus

It's a Battle

In the history of the Christian Church, every revival movement that started in grace and freedom, ended in law, institutionalism, and control. I believe it is because the leaders were naive about what they were up against. The grace-hating spirit took them out.

If you plan to start preaching grace in your church with the expectation that it's going to be easy – then don't even start! You need to realize how ferociously the enemy will oppose this message, and prepare yourself accordingly, or you will simply be eaten for breakfast by the grace-hating spirit. Martin Luther nearly lost his mind and he was often depressed. Can you imagine the resistance it arouses when one man steps out and says, "No!" to centuries of religious tradition? There has always been a small part of the Church that stood for salvation by grace, but it never really affected the mainstream Church, until Martin Luther decided to stand up and take the whole thing on. His stand provoked a massive response. While it may have manifested mainly through the Catholic Church, behind it all was the grace-hating spirit.

When you take a stand for the Gospel of Grace, the devil will notice and make sure you face opposition. That opposition does not even have to come through people, often it is an invisible hatred that comes on your mind – an invisible hostility.

I was in Hong Kong for at least a year before I preached for the first time on the finished work of the Cross. We caught the devil completely by surprise and the message just flowed, everyone received it and it was wonderful. I stepped out the pulpit, went home overjoyed, and then suddenly, out of nowhere, the heavens closed in. Such a spirit of heaviness came over me. Hong Kong wasn't used to hearing this message, and there was a reaction!

Please don't think that people were behind the reaction, it was the grace-hating spirit influencing them. Love the human beings, show mercy and kindness and don't react. Part of the enemy's strategy is that you get bitter and start fighting the people who oppose you. You start preaching to prove they are wrong and you are right, instead of preaching the Gospel. Jesus preached very strongly at the Pharisees and warned them, but he never reacted to their opposition. You need to have the courage to warn and rebuke people who preach against grace in your church, and the wisdom to see that the battle is being fought in the heavenly realms.

The grace-hating spirit will try to intimidate, undermine, tempt, and confuse you. It will do its utmost to make you compromise, or just quiet down. We see in Galatians 2, how even Peter succumbed to its onslaught: By the time he came to Paul's church in Antioch, he was overcome by the intimidation of the religious believers and joined them in their hypocrisy. Paul had the right and the courage to confront Peter.

Shepherds, you need to safeguard the Church from legalism! That is your main responsibility; to keep the Church free from the law. You can't rely on apostles to do that because many of them are under the law themselves.

I was under the law and I preached a mixture of law and grace from when I planted my first church more than thirty years ago in South Africa, until about six years ago, here in Hong Kong. I have resolved to never mix law and grace ever again. When you start preaching undiluted grace, "*spies, bewitchers, fear mongers, agitators, dogs, evil men, mutilators of the flesh, deceitful schemers,*" will appear seemingly out of thin air. At first, these people will come across friendly and smiling, but remember that legalism is fundamentally hypocritical, most legalists do not appear to be mean-hearted people, they are usually sweet and disarming. Do not be deceived by appearances though, they will disarm you from grace right into law. It is cunning, clever, deliberate, and intentional. Be aware!

I learnt in the military that you need to know your enemy, his strengths and weaknesses, his strategy and tactics, or he will wipe you out. Do not try to transition into grace naively thinking, "This is such a wonderful message and everyone is going to be happy!" No, you're going to face opposition. People are going to think you're crazy, that you've become a heretic. They're going to accuse you of things behind your back and there will be all sorts of gossip flying around. Behind all this is the grace-hating spirit, carefully coordinating its strategy to prevent the survival of the Gospel of Grace.

We are going to look at some of the faces of the grace-hating spirit, to equip you to be able to recognize the source of opposition and how to effectively stand in the face of it. One thing you can be sure of, opposition will come, but when you know its *modus operandi*, you will not be caught off guard.

Ugly Face 1: Opposition to Grace

> "Woe to you experts in the law, because you have taken away the key to knowledge. You yourselves have not entered, and you have hindered those who were entering."
>
> - Luke 11:52 (NIV)

There are leaders who are hindering their people from entering into the power and favor and blessing of God, hindering them from a revelation of the Gospel of Grace, because they themselves don't enter and they are preachers of a mixture of law and grace.

Jesus is grace! The law was given through Moses, grace and truth came in Jesus Christ. The law is impersonal, it was given through a mediation of angels through Moses, but Jesus, who is grace, came personally to the earth. Grace is not a doctrine – it is a person. His name is Jesus. Grace is His nature. That is the key to knowledge.

God is a god of grace. God never intended or desired to bring the law. Galatians 3 and Hebrews 10:8 make it clear that He brought the law because of Israel's unbelief.

> "When Jesus left there the Pharisees and the teachers of the law began to oppose Him..."
>
> - Luke 11:53

Religion and legalism will oppose Jesus, oppose grace. It will not enter into grace, and it will hinder others from entering.

Ugly Face 2: Fierce Opposition

The grace-hating spirit really is fierce! The Pharisees and teachers of the law,

> "...began to oppose Him fiercely."
>
> - Luke 11:53 (NIV)

If you have not yet felt it, then you have not been preaching grace the way that Paul preached it.

Grace himself faced fierce opposition, and the grace message will evoke the same ferocity.

Ugly Face 3: Lay Siege

They will lay siege against your ministry. During a siege, an opposing army encamps around your city and tries to stop supplies coming in and things going out.

They stop people listening to your preaching, or reading your books.

"You won't get invited to our camp."

"This will close doors to you."

Perhaps those are doors that should be closed. You might think that if you were more politically correct then those doors would be open. You shouldn't be going through doors that open because of political correctness. If you do, you will be compromising the Gospel at every turn.

> "...besiege Him with questions."
>
> - Luke 11:53 (NIV)

Questions are good, but questions within questions are not. That's why when people asked Jesus questions, sometimes He answered them beautifully, with sensitivity and grace, and sometimes He answered with a strong rebuke. He was not going to be a politically correct diplomat. The Gospel was too important.

Ugly Face 4: Entrapment

> "..waiting to catch him in something he might say."
>
> - Luke 11:53 (NIV)

The Pharisees caught that woman in adultery. It wasn't something they stumbled on. I believe they set her up. I personally think one of the Pharisees paid someone to commit adultery with her. They set her up and they caught her. When you start preaching this grace message you think, "I could be caught. I could fail. I could get into serious sin and if they caught me, what then? Then they really can control me!" Legalism makes sin go underground, but when they catch you they crucify you. Grace allows for sin to come out into the open, because there is an environment of love,

safety, accountability, and kindness.

The grace-hating spirit will set a trap to catch you. Grace communities should have the attitude that they are not looking to catch people out or be suspicious. That parable about logs and splinter has some relevance here. We ought not to be trying to catch people in sin. According to Galatians 5, we should restore a brother caught in sin, gently. Delighting in catching another in sin really shows an un-renewed, legalistic mindset. If someone does fall into sin and we find out, instead of catching them out, our job is to graciously and lovingly help them. There are certain sins you don't need to go public with, you just go to the Father. In 1 John, the Bible does say that we should confess our sins to one another, but only if you have sinned against someone! Confessing our sins applies only on a horizontal (human relationship) level, for the sake of relationship. As far as the Father is concerned, it is all gone and forgiven already.

Paul never wrote about confessing sins, not once! How could he if they are already gone, washed away by the blood? On the horizontal, however, I need to confess my faults or apologize to people I have wronged.

The grace-hating spirit is trying to catch you, laying in wait to ensnare you, working to besiege you. When you first start the transition into undiluted grace, the attacks will intensify for a while. Eventually, as you become more and more established in grace, that tyranny will diminish. You will find that no weapon formed against you can prosper and no tongue can rise up unchallenged.

Ugly Face No. 5: Spying

Spies are secretive. They hide. They are two faced and come amongst you for a hidden reason. They hide their real agenda, which is to exploit any opportunity where you are vulnerable and make you a slave to the law and to their control.

Paul went around releasing people from religious handcuffs, but spies came in right behind Paul, and put those handcuffs straight back on again. They brought 'balance' to the radical gospel Paul was preaching. You cannot balance grace with anything, especially not the law. They are contradictory, and there is no middle ground. The Gospel of Grace is a radical message, and you have to preach it that way, otherwise you're not preaching it.

People are hesitant to preach a radical Gospel of Grace, but have you ever thought how radical the law is? Those who preach a mixture of law and grace are actually just compromisers. If you are going to preach the law, do it properly. The full extent of the law requires that you cut your hand off if it's causing you to sin! When religious zealots fly planes into towers in the name of their god, they are being absolutely faithful to the law! Under the law, we should kill anyone who doesn't keep it! In fact, if you go read the law properly, you'll see that if your kids don't keep the law, then you must stone your own children. The reason why people say grace is radical is because they've never heard the law being taught properly.

About seven years ago, God gave me two years to study the law. I used to break out in a cold sweat every day. The law is frightening, it is extreme! That is why Christians shoot people at abortion clinics; they are being faithful to what they believe! Those who are more 'conservative', who preach a mixture of law and grace, are actually just compromisers, backslidden legalists. They just preach the more palatable, more do-able parts of the law. They water down law and water down grace and eventually people don't know the difference.

Preach the law properly and then preach the fullness of grace and see how people will respond! They will say, "I am out of here - this is schizophrenic!" These things are so radically different that they cannot meet! It is only because the Church has preached a watered down version of the law and of grace for more than a thousand years, that people today allow themselves to sit under a compromised mish-mash of the ministry of life and the ministry of death.

A few fools for Jesus are going to have to stand up and take on this grace-hating spirit. Just as Martin Luther took it on, I am taking it on! There have been many times when Glenda and I have fallen into each other's arms, weeping. There have been times when Glenda has said; "Oh Rob, please stop! You are calling fire on our heads."

Martin Luther didn't have a choice. Once he had a glimpse of grace, he was finished. Once you see this, you are finished. You are ruined to the law forever.

I have been to conferences where they preach the law, and while they are preaching, I sit there and think, "I am so sorry, but I am getting angry. Oh Lord, I repent, I repent! But look at all these people becoming more and more confused!" I can't just sit there quietly any more! Either I have to go to the leaders and ask them if they know what they are doing, or I just have to leave. I pray that every minister who is preaching a mixture of law and grace will see this revelation and repent to their people.

> "[4] This matter arose because some false believers had infiltrated our ranks to spy on the freedom we have in Christ Jesus and to make us slaves. [5] We did not give in to them for a moment, so that the truth of the gospel might be preserved for you."
>
> - Galatians 2:4-5 (NIV)

Here we see their goal, their agenda: To spy on our freedom and make us slaves. Note the apostolic passion of Paul's response:

"We did not give in to them for a moment!"

Paul knew that giving in would be a threat to the Gospel itself. This is why it is imperative that we not give in, even for a moment.

I preached in Cape Town to two thousand people a night a few years ago. There were hundreds and hundreds of hungry people there, but there were also spies in the camp, spies checking me out. I could feel them in the crowd. Prophetic people experience this all the time; they can feel when there are spies around. Jesus could! We see in Matthew 9 and 12, and in Luke 12, that Jesus, "knew their thoughts". I could feel the spies there. God even showed me who some of them were, and some of them shouldn't have been spies!

People for who the message of grace is a new thing, and who are therefore evaluating the message and grappling with it, are not spies That is fine, even good! I am talking about individuals who come with the express purpose of trying to catch you, waiting for you to say something that they can twist and distort, something they can use against you. Those are spies!

So because I could discern so many spies in the crowd, I said to the brothers I was with; "Now listen, if I preach in Hong Kong, then I can be as naughty as I like, that is my turf and my jurisdiction, but here I am a guest on someone else's turf. I am accountable to those leaders and I can't just do anything I want. If I start getting naughty because of the spies out there, show me by code signals. I want to cross every 't' and dot every 'i' theologically, and leave no gap for these spies to seize." My daughter, Bonnie, came to me afterwards and asked me if something was wrong, because I had been so tame, so disciplined during my sermon. Some of the elders in the church which was hosting the event told me later that they had never heard the Gospel of Grace being laid out so clearly. Some of them who had a few reservations about parts of the grace message I was preaching, said after this, "That is it – we can't argue."

I worked really hard at that event so that there would be nothing I said that the enemy could distort, or use out of context. But even so, some spies went back to their home churches and announced, "Rob is preaching that you don't have to submit to leaders, and you can sin as much as you like." After this I realized that it is not a rational thing, but the grace-hating spirit. Those spies don't know what they are doing to their congregations. Members of those congregations, who had known me for years, e-mailed me and asked me whether what they had heard was true. We wrote back and clarified what we had said, and they told us that they always believed that what their pastor said wasn't true, because they knew me. At least they checked out those rumors.

Leaders who are fighting this message don't know that they are fighting God. While it is important to be accountable, we have to preach grace boldly. Do not give in to those spies, even for a moment!

Ugly Face No. 6: A Bewitching Spirit

"You foolish Galatians - who has bewitched you?"

- Galatians 3:1 (NIV)

Today, witchcraft is being preached in churches around the world. Christ died to remove the law forever, and when anyone preaches law, it cannot be the Holy Spirit who empowers them to preach what Christ has removed. It must be another spirit – a spirit of witchcraft.

The disciples wanted to call fire down on the Samaritans and Jesus rebuked them saying, "*You are of the wrong spirit.*" In the same way, legalists will call fire down on the world, announcing that God is killing, judging, and smashing. He isn't! There is a day of judgment coming but, "*In the last days I will pour out my Spirit (for salvation) on all flesh.*" God's agenda is salvation, not judgment.

We are dealing with occultic powers that are in the Church. The devil doesn't invest much time or resources in those we traditionally call witches, with black cats and broomsticks, – that is just his hobby. In the Church, the main agenda of witchcraft is to bring believers under law. He is the accuser of the brethren. If he accuses you enough, if you are under even a little bit of law, he will pour such condemnation on you that before you know it, you are placing yourself under more law to try and improve your condemned state, and the freedom and joy you once had in Christ is suddenly nowhere to be found. That's called witchcraft.

Ugly Face No. 7: Fear

Have you ever experienced a sudden fear of being caught out, or of being found out? You hear a message on that old style holiness (which is not real holiness at all – it is still legalism dressed up as holiness), or someone comes among you and you can't help feeling that they are more holy than you, because they don't go to movies or don't drink wine, and you feel fear. You're afraid that they might find out how unholy you are, because you do drink wine or go to the movies. You involuntarily start agreeing with them and their standards! You find yourself acting as if those things are evil, or somehow only for second-rate Christians, and you would never do them. That fear is causing you to rebuild the law over your life, and to make out that Christ is the one doing the rebuilding. You become a hypocrite and confuse those in freedom because you change your behavior when certain people are in your midst.

If Peter, who had open visions of Heaven and clear revelation of the Gospel, could go back under law because of fear of the legalists, then it is

obvious that we are not dealing with any logical thing, but a spirit of fear. An intimidating spirit that uses fear to bring about control.

Ugly Face no. 8: The agitators

> "When Peter came to Antioch, I opposed him to his face. He was clearly in the wrong…because he was afraid of those who belonged to the circumcision group ... so that by their hypocrisy even Barnabas was led astray... in front of them all I said; 'How is it that you force Gentiles to follow Jewish customs?'"
>
> - Galatians 2:11-14 (NIV)

> "You were running a good race, who cut in on you to keep you from obeying the truth."
>
> - Galatians 5:7 (NIV)

Peter was one of the big boys. I'm not sure I'd have the courage to oppose someone like Peter! I think Paul was so passionate about the Gospel, that it overcame his fear. Paul said to Peter that he wasn't acting in line with the truth of the Gospel. Obeying the truth isn't obeying the law, it is acting in line with the truth of the Gospel.

When Peter changed from eating food in freedom, to only eating Kosher food, he was not acting in line with the Gospel. Now, if they were trying to break into a Jewish community, I guarantee you, Paul would have been right there with Peter, eating Kosher food, in order to reach those Jews. But they were in a church which was free from all that stuff, Jews and Gentile believers alike. The Jews coming up from Jerusalem were not unsaved Jews, they were born-again Jews who should have known better! Can you see the difference? There's tolerance to the unsaved, we become all things for the sake of winning them to Christ. But in this case, it was not tolerance. A Christian who considers himself to be strong and mature in faith, who cannot handle you drinking or not drinking wine, is not mature, but a Pharisee.

"We don't eat certain foods offered to idols." Paul says it doesn't make one bit of difference. I can walk into demon temples and eat anything, because I know who is on the inside of me, and what the blood of Jesus did. I got saved in a Hindu temple, for goodness sake! That's where I met Jesus! That is why I love going into temples; it reminds me of where I got saved. There were idols in that temple, I had my head shaved, I wore saffron robe, and Jesus came into a Hindu temple and I got saved! So I'm happy in a Hindu temple.

Some Christians, on the other hand, think those demons are bigger than their God. They are weak in faith, let's honor that. I wouldn't go into a temple if I knew someone was weak in faith, but at the same time, Paul wrote that we could eat food offered to idols and enjoy it! He said there is a demon behind every idol, but to eat and enjoy it, even if it's been offered to a demon! The moment you touch it, it's sanctified! But he said to those who are weak in faith, that they should refuse to eat that food rather than undermine their faith. So those born-again Jews who came up from Jerusalem, who had been set free from the law and were eating non-kosher food, should never have gone back to only eating kosher food. Paul said to them twice that they were not acting in line with the truth, they were being hypocrites. Their agenda with the Galatians was to get them to obey the law again, and Paul writes that if they had been able to get the Galatians to come under the law again, the Galatians would no longer be obeying the truth. To go back under the law is to be disobedient to the truth of the Gospel.

> "as for those agitators, I wish they would go the whole way and emasculate themselves!"
>
> - Galatians 3:12 (NIV)

We had a Jack Russell in Australia; he was a magnificent specimen. We used to sit and watch TV together. He was serious about watching TV; he would sit on the chair next to me with his back against the back rest and his paws up, like a human. From time to time, a blue tongue lizard would come into our garden. They are very ferocious and strong, but because of Skabenga, our dog, they never lasted long. He would catch them and rip them apart. He would bite them behind the neck and violently shake them from side to side with incredible strength and ferocity. After only a few seconds, there would be pieces of dead reptile all over. Skabenga's chest would be covered in blood, and he'd come over to me and drop the shredded carcass at my feet. That is exactly what the goal of an agitator is; to rip you to shreds, to agitate you so much that you don't know whether you're coming or going. You start disintegrating in confusion.

Ugly Face no. 9: Dogs, Evil Men, Mutilators

> "[1] It is no trouble for me to write the same things to you again, and it is a safeguard for you. [2] Watch out for those dogs, those evildoers, those mutilators of the flesh."
>
> - Philippians 3:1-2 (NIV)

It's important to see that Paul doesn't mind reminding them of certain things again, because it's a safeguard for them. We too, should do this. Preach grace, preach a series on grace, preach it again, and preach it again, because it's a safeguard. The Church needs to be safeguarded.

Let's take a look at what the Church needs to be safeguarded from. I believe the Church is not being safeguarded because of the absence of authentic apostolic ministry in the earth. There are many apostles around, but I guarantee you, all that calls itself apostolic, is not. The credentials of an apostle; signs, wonders, and miracles, should be a major part of their life and ministry. If that's not a major thrust of their life, they might be an apostle, but they're not operating in their gift. Wherever apostles go, churches will be planted. Even when we talk about 'marketplace apostles', somewhere along the line, churches have to be planted. Communities that embody grace, where elders have been appointed into leadership, should be found somewhere in the trail of an apostle. Apostles will safeguard the Church against legalism, denominationalism, popery, and institutionalism. If they're not safeguarding the Church, they're not operating as apostles.

What was Paul working to safeguard the Church from, by reminding them of certain things again?

> "...watch out for those dogs, those men who do evil, those mutilators of the flesh."

(The Jewish nation used to call gentiles dogs, now a Jewish apostle is calling Jewish legalists, dogs!)

What kinds of things were those "dogs" doing?

> "[4] If someone else thinks they have reasons to put confidence in the flesh, I have more: [5] circumcised on the eighth day, of the people of Israel, of the tribe of Benjamin, a Hebrew of Hebrews; in regard to the law, a Pharisee; [6] as for zeal, persecuting the church; as for righteousness based on the law, faultless. [7] But whatever were gains to me I now consider loss for the sake of Christ. [8] What is more, I consider everything a loss because of the surpassing worth of knowing Christ Jesus my Lord, for whose sake I have lost all things. I

> consider them garbage, that I may gain Christ [9] and be found in him, not having a righteousness of my own that comes from the law, but that which is through faith in Christ—the righteousness that comes from God on the basis of faith."
>
> - Philippians 3:4-9 (NIV)

Those "*evil workers*" were preaching a confidence in the flesh, preaching law, and Paul calls them dogs. Historically, the Church hasn't been safe-guarded from these men. If you want to see the end result of not being safeguarded from these evil workers, just take a look at extreme fundamen-talist religions and see how the women are being treated, how they treat non-conforming members, their forms of discipline, etc. Fundamentalist Christian groups are just as bad, they just work more subtly. The fallout rate in the church world is shocking. The world is strewn with millions of Christians that are hurt, broken, and devastated by condemnation. Some might wonder what is there in the law to be safeguarded from, after all, the law is holy. But Paul calls those men *dogs, mutilators of the flesh, evil workers.* As long as the Church refuses to confront these legalists, the controllers carry on controlling, and the Popes keep giving Papal decrees and violating lo-cal church autonomy. Christians in many cultures today are so loyal they don't want to question anything, they feel they must obey orders. It's time to stop allowing yourself to be controlled, disobey those orders! You're not a rebel. There's a thin line between being a rebel and a non-conformist. I don't want to be a rebel, because rebellion is like witchcraft, but I want to be a non-conformist. Not everyone who disagrees with what man is lead-ing into is rebellious.

I teach our church that there are four levels of authority; The first is God, His manifest glory, a revelation of His nature. Every believer must know that the number one authority is God himself!

The second authority is His Word, third is the believer's conscience, and fourth is leadership! In many places I've seen leaders above God, above His Word and above the believer's conscience. This is especially true if you come from a regimented society like South Africa or China. If you go to the bank, for example, and ask a question about something that isn't inside the normal scope of things, inside the box of the person you are talking to, they have to go up to someone above them. Everything is referred up the chain of command, no one will take the initiative. This isn't wrong in itself, but those societies are more vulnerable to being controlled.

Why would an intelligent, educated man like Paul use such horrifically offensive words to describe preachers of the law, and say that the Church needs to be safeguarded from them and their teaching? Do you think leaders around the world are awake to this issue? I don't think so, because that is why control, institutionalism, and guilt manipulation is happening right across so much of the church world.

We need to teach believers the proper levels of authority, because most Christians today are so prone to manipulation and seduction. Some of the Chinese people in our church were like that when they first joined us. In Hong Kong, Christians tend to go to every Christian conference and every guest speaker who visits Hong Kong. I never told anyone not to go to a certain conference or not to listen to certain preachers. I did, however, preach the Gospel of Grace over and over and over again. Now, those same Christians come to me after attending some conference or going to see some visiting preacher, and tell me about how they see how that speaker preaches manipulation and law.

I've heard that bank tellers get so used to the feel of real money, that when they come across a counterfeit note, they can feel it immediately. C.H. Spurgeon said that we should stop trying to preach against every possible counterfeit, but simply let the Lion of the Tribe of Judah out of his cage, and His roar will deal with those things. Preach the real Gospel to your people, and you won't need to cage them with laws and boundaries to try and protect them or keep them in line. Our people can go to conferences, they can walk into temples, they can discern for themselves. They're mature enough that if they do listen to a message filled with legalism, they are able to pick out the meat and simply throw out the bones.

Ugly Face no. 10: Deceitful Schemers

"[1] As a prisoner for the Lord, then, I urge you to live a life worthy of the calling you have received. [2] Be completely humble and gentle; be patient, bearing with one another in love. [3] Make every effort to keep the unity of the Spirit through the bond of peace. [4] There is one body and one Spirit, just as you were called to one hope when you were called; [5] one Lord, one faith, one baptism; [6] one God and Father of all, who is over all and through all and in all. [7] But to each one of us grace has been given as Christ apportioned it. [8] This is why it says:

'When he ascended on high,
he took many captives
and gave gifts to his people.'

[9] (What does 'he ascended' mean except that he also descended to the lower, earthly regions? [10] He who descended is the very one who ascended higher than all the heavens, in order to fill the whole universe.) [11] So Christ himself gave the apostles, the prophets, the evangelists, the pastors and teachers, [12] to equip his people for works of service, so that the body of Christ may be built up [13] until we all reach unity in the faith and in the knowledge of the Son of God and become mature, attaining to the whole measure of the fullness of Christ.

> [14] Then we will no longer be infants, tossed back and forth by the waves, and blown here and there by every wind of teaching and by the cunning and craftiness of people in their deceitful scheming. [15] Instead, speaking the truth in love, we will grow to become in every respect the mature body of him who is the head, that is, Christ. [16] From him the whole body, joined and held together by every supporting ligament, grows and builds itself up in love, as each part does its work."
>
> - Ephesians 4:1-16

Apostles, prophets, pastors, teachers, and evangelists of the New Covenant impart grace gifts, just as their gifting was by grace. It's their impartation of grace which will take the Church from the unity of the spirit, a unity which comes from all being under one Lord, of one faith, and one baptism, to unity in the faith and knowledge of the Son of God.

We are encouraged to make every effort to maintain the unity of the spirit. As those who are born-again, it doesn't matter what you believe, there is unity at this level. But the grace gifting of the five-fold ascension gifts is to bring people into such a knowledge of Jesus, that we come to the unity at a whole new and infinitely higher level, and attain the fullness of the stature of Christ.

Now, there's going to be opposition to us coming into the full stature of Christ. That is why we can't afford to have apostles, prophets, pastors, teachers, and evangelists who don't know this message of grace, or we'll never come into the full measure. At this point, "*we will no longer be infants, blown by every wind of teaching.*" Notice that Paul didn't write, "by every wind of error", but, "*by every wind of teaching, and by the cunning and craftiness of men, in their deceitful scheming.*"

There comes a time when the five-fold ministers have completed their work in a local church, because it can now build itself up. It's a mature

church that has come to the stature of Christ, its members are building each other up, the royal priesthood of God!

A local church which is associated with these ministers or ministries can come to the full stature of Christ, and ultimately build itself up. There isn't a church I'm aware of in the world today that has achieved this. But I believe that the grace revolution sweeping the globe is a prophetic sign of our wonderful sovereign Lord's intention. The manifest wisdom of God will be revealed through a Church that has matured to reflect the full measure of the stature of Christ. If you are reading this book, it is very likely that you have joined in this journey of grace inspired adventure.

I don't have to be a prophet to know the chances are that you have already encountered some of these ugly faces of the grace-hating spirit. I would like to say to you, "Well done!" Whatever scars, or pain, or times of loneliness you may have suffered, Heaven salutes you, and I, amongst many others, applaud you! Don't give up because of the opposition you have faced. Instead, lift up your eyes, for there is one face so glorious, and which shines with such pleasure towards you, that it makes everything so wonderfully worthwhile! The end result is guaranteed: Nations and multitudes liberated to adore the Lamb that was slain, and who lives forever. Worthy is the Lamb!

CHAPTER 5

Grace and Leadership

by Fini de Gersigny

For those on the journey of grace, leadership is such a vital ingredient in the restoration of this truth to the Church. Leaders, especially the lead couple, set the tone, DNA, and theology in the life of a local church. I find this a somewhat daunting proposition, as well as a great joy, since as the Lord gets hold of us and transforms us; the flow-on effect to the local church is stunning. Paul wrote,

> "Therefore, I urge you to imitate me."
>
> - 1 Corinthians 4:16 (NIV)

If leaders are full of grace, it stands to reason that our grace walk will become the grace walk of those following us. The opposite is true as well, if leaders are insecure, easily threatened, and have to lead through control and legalism, that makes for a pretty toxic family. Grace is more than a powerful message; it is a personal encounter with Jesus and a revelation of the finished work of the Cross. It is Jesus ministering in the power of the Holy Spirit at the express will of the Father. We can pick up on a grace message and change our church language without having an encounter with the Person of grace. However, this will not produce long lasting fruit and life.

I discovered how grace-less I was almost 10 years ago. One night, as I was putting one of my children to bed, he said to me, "Dad, I'll never be good enough for you." Wow! That was a heart stopping moment. I was struck to the core with the depth of what I was communicating to my family, and of course this would have been filtering into the church as well. *If grace is not lived out at home, then it certainly won't be lived out in the church community.* I realized that I was living out my own core belief system, which was based on performance indicators. Those indicators can be all the "right" things, like personal prayer, devotion, holiness, love, etc. and yet our motivation behind keeping them is not grace, but the law. And so those closest to you, and those you are ministering to and with, constantly feel a low-grade disapproval, even though you really want to encourage and release them.

So I will recount some of the key revelations on my grace journey, and law-detox, which will hopefully help and encourage you to flourish and enjoy the rest of your leadership years.

1. The Father Is Already Pleased with Me, Irrespective of What I Do or Do Not Achieve with My Life and Ministry

> "And the Holy Spirit descended upon Him in bodily form, like a dove, and a voice came from heaven, saying 'You are my Son, the Beloved! In You I am well pleased and find delight.'"
>
> - Luke 3:22 (Amp)

The Father was delighted with Jesus *before* he had begun his ministry, worked miracles, taught the multitudes, or paid the ultimate price on the Cross. This is an encounter with the *unconditional acceptance and love of the Father* that every leader needs to experience, or else the *basis* of their ministry will be to try and please God, people, or both. By 'being loved by God', I mean intoxicated, wooed, overwhelmed, drunk with his love personally, and not just as a one-off revelation. I believe we can go so deep into the love of God that when people come near us they will feel this love spilling over.

I find myself looking forward to Sundays, not just because I love ministering, but because I know I am going to be ministered to by the love of God during our congregational worship. Sometimes I get so caught up in his love and grace that I have to pull myself back to reality so that I can try to work out what we should do next!

How you feel about yourself and your acceptance as a leader, son, daughter, and human being, will ultimately impact what you minister to

others. My success is not based on the size of my church, how many people I have baptized this year, or the number of healings we have had. The Father is already pleased with me and *loves* me now, just as I am, and *before* I go out and do amazing exploits in his name.

I lead, not out of a need to please the Father, he's already pleased with me, but out of my secure calling to be the leader I know He has called me to be. I've told my children that they have a 'love tank' that needs to be constantly filled with hugs, kisses and cuddles. They come to me regularly for love tank refills. This is not unlike our love walk with the Father, where we are able to regularly sit/walk/worship in His presence and have our love tanks filled, for no reason other than just to enjoy Him!

He loves to love on us, and I make no apology for needing His love. Leadership can be traumatic at times, and without frequent encounters with God's love and presence, I don't think I would have made it this far. Leaders who have not been loved on by the Father, won't have much to give their flock other than principles and patterns and Bible verses. Jesus was so full of love and was so secure in the Father's love that it poured out of His every pore. I want to be that full. I want to be that secure.

2. His Yoke Is Easy and His Burden Is Light

I read a quote recently that went something like, "If you haven't found the place where ministry is fun, then do yourself and all those around you a favor, quit now." Well, a few years ago I would have glared at you with resentment just for thinking that ministry could be fun! I was so conditioned to 'the price of the ministry', that I would have defended my grim demeanor, and even found some scriptures to defend my gloom! How far from the truth this is.

Jesus said that we should take *His* yoke, which is *easy*, and *His* burden, which is *light*! (Matthew 11:30). Some Christians are so burdened by the ministry that you don't really want to be around them, because you feel guilty you aren't more 'burdened' by a love for the lost, or desire to plant more churches. Yet you wouldn't really want to be like them, because they don't really look very happy and their spouses look positively worn out!

My life has its fair share of pressures, trials, suffering, persecutions, and the like. But when you are in a joyful frame of mind about ministry, it's so much easier to tackle the challenges that ministry will throw at you. "*The joy of the Lord is our strength.*" Jesus was "*full of joy in the Holy Spirit,*" and I believe His leaders and ministers have every opportunity to live and minister from a place of overflowing joy.

We don't know *exactly* what Paul meant when he said he wanted to "*share in the fellowship of Christ's sufferings*" (Philippians 3:10), but I asked the Lord, and I felt He said to me that those sufferings are the sufferings you didn't cause, but that come as a by-product of following Him: persecution, trials, 'sheep bites', and the like. We can get through these sorts of sufferings best with a disposition of joy.

If we preach freedom but live lives of burden and somberness, that's just hypocrisy. I have always been an overly responsible and disciplined person. Unfortunately, these admirable traits don't always translate into overflowing fun! I think my family suffered the most from my dedicated grim and fun-less demeanor. And I attribute a lot of my lack of joy in those days to my overly responsible preoccupation with the church and ministry, and the rarity of my personal encounters with God and His loving grace. I think many leaders suffer from this. They know in theory that Jesus is building His Church, but they allow the pressure, responsibilities and even godly zeal, to rob them of their childlike joy in the ministry.

These days I look forward to staff meetings, healing rooms, leadership

retreats, Sunday services, and all the many other aspects of church ministry. There is a joy in my heart and a spring in my step. Some staff meetings end with a good number of us on the floor, rolling with laughter. Is it perfect? Not at all. It's just more happy than not! I used to be burdened by whether people stayed at the church or left, whether there would be enough money for salaries, whether the meetings would go well, etc. The more I worried the more grim I looked! I am not saying that nowadays I just don't care if someone sees fit to leave Jubilee and go somewhere else. If I was close to them I might have a sense of loss, but I just don't take it all so personally, as though their leaving is a reflection of how I am performing as a leader! This is a tyranny no one should live under. Do I get all the credit for all those who stay and build with us? Not often. So why should I shoulder all the blame for those who move on?

If Jesus is really building His Church, like He said He would, then even when I am sleeping, the job is being done and I don't need to be weighed down by all these burdens, because His yoke is easy (Greek: *chrestos – useful, good, manageable, pleasant, kind)* and His burden is light (Greek: *elaphros – light in weight, quick, agile).*

3. Operate in the Grace Gift that You've Been Given

> "Each one should use whatever gift he has received to serve others, faithfully administering God's grace in its various forms."
>
> - 1 Peter 4:10 (NIV)

> "I became a servant of this gospel by the gift of God's grace given me through the working of his power."
>
> - Ephesians 3:8 (NIV)

> "But by the grace of God I am what I am."
>
> - 1 Corinthians 15:10 (NIV)

The gifts of pastor, teacher, apostle, administrator, psalmist, etc. are just that, *grace gifts.* There is an ease and grace to ministry when you are a square peg operating in a square hole. I have wished at times that I had some of the skills and gifts that others operate in so easily and naturally, because I felt that if I somehow had more skill, then my church would grow and I would be more "successful". What a tyranny! Firstly, *success* is simply being everything God has called you to be. We have six children but we are not more "successful" than someone who has two!

The size of our church is not related to whether we are successful or not. You could have a sizable church, but if you are driven and grumpy, are you really successful? I think we are successful when we are simply doing what God has called us to do with grace and love. It is obviously more fun to shepherd a growing church, but I believe I was successful before Jubilee really started to grow.

Whenever we compare ourselves to someone else, we are usually measuring our deficiencies, and it is not the Father's will to live life in someone else's shadow. When we are content in what the Lord has called us to, and appreciate the way He has wired us, then we will be so much easier to live with, and so much more content as leaders! When I look at the leaders who have emerged around me, I see people who are different to me in many ways, but we celebrate that diversity and it makes us, and the body, that much stronger. Be the best *you* can be. Celebrate who you are, love how God has made you!

> "A man can only receive what is given him from heaven."
>
> - John 3:27 (NIV)

> "I have learned the secret of being content in any and every situation…"

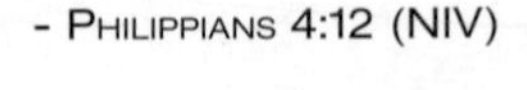

- Philippians 4:12 (NIV)

4. Work on Your Strengths and Not Your Weaknesses

For years I lived under the lie that I should be "working on my weaknesses". Somehow, after years of diligent working, some of my weaknesses were even weaker. (I am not talking here about character flaws or morality.) Then a book by John Maxwell liberated me, when I read that my *strengths* were why people drove across town and past many other good churches to come to Jubilee.

Since then, I have been working on my strengths and allowing the Lord to simply raise up people around me who are strong where I am weak. There is a huge freedom in this, as many leaders live under the misconception that we have to "be everything to everyone". This is just not true or sustainable. No one can live under that yoke, it will wear you out.

God wired my wife, Isi, and me in a certain way, and so my family and our church will look like something that comes out of our heart DNA. I can't look at other leaders, churches, or ministries and try to emulate them, or wish we could do things they're doing. I need to be myself and let that freedom affect every ministry around me. Down the road from us is one of the most famous churches in the world. We love them and honor them, but feel no pressure whatsoever to be like them. Many leaders look at Jubilee and appreciate our DNA, and some visit and take some of that DNA back with them to their congregations. Ultimately though, each church has a unique thumbprint and true freedom is enjoying yourself and how the Lord has wired you.

I encourage our small group leaders to develop their groups around their strengths. One may be very hospitable, and so food and fellowship will be a major element of that group. Another may be very prophetic and musical, and so worship and prophecy will be a major element in that group. In this way, ministering in the *grace* God has given us will allow us to minister with *longevity,* and avoid the burnout that so often characterizes leaders in ministry.

A good example of this is my wife, Isi. For years she lived under the yoke of "pastors wife", whatever that is! As a result, she functioned in a fraction of her capacity, because the apostolic structure we were in did not have a grid for female governmental prophets (which she clearly was and is). She was able to function only as a psalmist, but she was unable to share or minister out of many of her insights into the glory realm, revelations while caught up into the third heaven, or visions, dreams and trances, etc. because the wineskin could not cope with it.

In her transformation, the first person who needed to repent (change their thinking) was me! Growing up in a misogynistic culture did not help me to see my greatest gift and ally, right under my nose. Our marriage needed a major work-over and I needed a revelation of just how amazing a "helper" the Lord had given me. It has taken some years for this to fully work its way out, but I can truly say today that she is flying in the gifts and callings the Lord has given her, without any stigma to her gender. She is much more of a visionary elder than I am at times, and I am totally comfortable with that. We work together as a team and now that these issues are settled, we accomplish so much more. What that looks like in day-to-day ministry is that we consult together on everything. We pray together, we work to each other's strengths. Sometimes I take a stronger lead and other times she does, depending on the situation and season. It's really still a work in progress, but we are determined to listen to the Holy Spirit and each other and try to have as much fun as possible on the way.

What are your strengths? Work on them. Be happy with who you are and those you minister to will become happy too. *Happy leaders, happy sheep!*

5. Work with People You Choose

> "He appointed twelve – designating them apostles – that they might be with him."
>
> - Mark 3:14 (NIV)

Jesus had the prerogative of choosing His disciples and He called them to "*be with him*". While we know from the Gospels that they were all on a steep learning curve, they were happy and privileged to be with Him, and He was happy to have them along for the mentoring journey, often delegating and entrusting major outreaches and missions to them.

His ultimate vote of confidence in the disciples was delegating them to launch the Church that bore His name! There are few things that will sap the strength of a leader more, than working with people who undermine, sulk, baulk, whinge, or generally just get in the way of where you feel the Lord is taking you.

I had a dysfunctional leadership like this for several years, comprising people who did all of the above, and sadly I accepted this as my lot in life. I resigned myself to this sad status quo. Many elders' meetings were a chore rather than a delight. Being called to the front line of ministry is tough enough, without having to share the trenches with people who neither really trust you or like you, and in fact might even shoot a few arrows your way if they get a chance!

This is pure dysfunction, and not the Kingdom of Heaven. Heaven is harmony, honor, joy, peace, and unity. After a painful church split some years ago, (Jesus did have Judas on His team!). We have been able to rebuild our staff and leadership team with people who we like and who like us. They are gifted, but we do not hold their gifting in disproportionate weight to our ability to just enjoy their company and know that they honor

us, are shield bearers, and are watching our back, just as we do the same for them.

What a different culture and atmosphere we have now: It is grace filled, releasing and empowering all at the same time. I am not watching my back any more, while at the same time we have developed a culture where leaders can speak their minds on any subject, without the fear of being shot down in flames.

The buck stops with Isi and me, and we wear that comfortably because His yoke is easy. And we have a gifted team around us that make us look far more successful than we really are! Within our close staff and pastoral team we demand humility and transparency. What that looks like, is that sometimes there is very vulnerable and honest sharing of hearts and lives. It looks like prayer and prophetic encounters together. At other times it looks like Acts 2 Holy Spirit commotion. The DNA of our team will transfer to every part of the body so we keep everything in the light.

6. Lead without Apology

"The elders who direct the affairs of the church well..."

- 1 Timothy 5:17 (NIV)

The Lord Jesus is expecting elders to direct the affairs of the Church *well.* And I believe that the father and mother of the work need to direct the affairs of the eldership team well. They might have different titles in different Church contexts; Senior Pastors, Visionary Elders, Lead Elders, etc. but the title is not as important as the anointing and function. Throughout history, both biblical history and Church history, God has always used strong leaders to accomplish His purposes. A leader will always have to pay a price to stand in that front line position. Yet, the way they tackle their task needs to be built on a foundation of accepting what God has called them to do, that is, to *lead*.

I think in some grace circles there is the misconception that to be a grace leader, you must become a push over: a fuzzy, warm, congenial nice guy who offends no one. When a leader comes out of an autocratic wineskin, he can sometimes swing to the other extreme of weak leadership. Neither extreme is a healthy one.

Jesus was the perfect leader. He admonished His disciples and He demanded humility and integrity. He did not tolerate the religious spirit nor did He bow to popular opinion or corporate expectations. He followed the direction of the Father in the power of the Holy Spirit. He loved, rebuked and corrected His disciples in equal measure. He was not intimidated, and at no point felt the need to pander to, or be popular with, those He led. And yet, John was so relaxed and secure with Jesus' love that he leant on His chest at the last supper. Jesus somehow kept the balance of leader and family. His disciples were constantly aware of His love and servant heart, yet were also happily submitted to His direction. I am sure Peter felt a bit bruised after being admonished with "*get behind me Satan!*" and yet a good leader knows how to encourage and correct in balanced proportion. If we're correcting more than encouraging, we'll run out of followers!

Paul, the grace champion, does not mince his words either; encouraging the elders to warn divisive people, hand one person over to Satan and "*command*" the wealthy to be generous. To balance this, though, we see elders always appearing in Paul's writing in the plural. A team of elders is more likely to hear the heart of God on a matter than an isolated dictator. I don't believe eldership is a round table, where everyone has an equal say either. While I believe we are all equal before the Lord, there is a weight, of both responsibility and authority resting on the lead couple, where they will have to make a final decision, one way or another, once they have heard and taken cognizance of the elders' input. It would be a foolish se-

nior leader who would consistently ignore the input of his team. No one needs a team of 'yes men'. Our elders need to be leaders of stature and anointing, prayer, and the Word, able to discern doctrinal issues, and do it in a way that is *full of grace.*

The eldership team needs to be a tightly knit band of friends who have each other's best interest at heart. They are in love with Jesus and love each other deeply, and so would never do anything to hurt or damage the family fabric of the Church.

7. Fathers and Sons

> "See, I will send you the prophet Elijah before that great and dreadful day of the Lord comes. He will turn the hearts of the fathers to their children, and the hearts of the children to their fathers; or else I will come and strike the land with a curse."
>
> - Malachi 4:5 (NIV)

Family is so important in regard to grace leadership. For too long, sections of the Church have adopted a business model for church life with a management structure lifted from the corporate world. This is inherently dangerous, for in it are the seeds wherein people can become a conveyance for personal kingdom building, instead of the fathers and sons of Bible culture, building the Kingdom of Heaven.

Where there is successful generational succession you will always see the father/son principal in action:

- Joshua was a successor to Moses.
- Samuel was a spiritual mentor to David.
- Elisha succeeded Elijah.
- Ruth was a daughter to Naomi.
- Timothy was a son to the apostle Paul.

I could also list the failures of many biblical leaders to raise spiritual sons, resulting in a backslidden Israel, or a ministry that just petered out.

At the tender age of 19, when I became an elder in the church Rob Rufus led, I had the joy of learning many of the deep truths and convictions that I hold to today through friendship, training, correction, and example. Rob and I remain best friends after more than 30 years of co-laboring in God. The sons become fathers to their father's delight.

> "[19] I hope in the Lord Jesus to send Timothy to you soon, that I also may be cheered when I receive news about you. [20] I have no one else like him, who takes a genuine interest in your welfare. [21] For everyone looks out for his own interests, not those of Jesus Christ. [22] But you know that Timothy has proved himself, because as a son with his father he has served with me in the work of the gospel."
>
> - Philippians 2:19-22 (NIV)

Paul worked with many co-laborers during his many years of ministry, but singles out only Timothy for this commendation. Timothy had those qualities that stand out in a son:

- He was passionate in the cause of Christ and His kingdom.
- He was passionate about the same things that Paul was passionate – in this instance, the welfare of the Philippian Church.
- He was loyal to Paul himself and represented him well, to the extent that Paul indicated that sending Timothy was like him going himself.
- Timothy was trained, then empowered and released by Paul. This process clearly took years.

Other traits we can see in developing true sons in the Lord:

- Sons honor their fathers, if they can't do it to this degree, it's just a job. Ruth 1:16

- Spiritual sons are hungrier for God and his presence than anything else. Joshua remained in the presence of God long after Moses had left. Exodus 33:11
- Sons watch the fathers. This was true of Jesus who "*only did what he saw the Father doing*", and also of Elisha who had to keep his eyes on Elijah if he was to receive his mantle and double anointing. John 5:19; 2 Kings 2:10
- Sonship cannot be imposed or coerced. It is by mutual agreement and co-operation. Sons need fathers and the fathers need sons. "*The son can do nothing by himself.*" John 5:19
- Sons become fathers in their own right and it's crucial to recognize when the transition has taken place, or otherwise the relationship can sour.
- Sons hopefully go on to exceed their fathers' accomplishments. Elisha performs twice the miracles his spiritual father Elijah performed. Jesus promised His disciples that through the power of the Holy Spirit that they would do *greater* works than He had done. It seems that He was really excited about His disciples fulfilling this word.

Several years ago I heard someone ask Bill Johnson what he felt the Lord was doing in the earth. I was expecting an answer that would include revival, signs and wonders, etc. Bill's answer, "*Raising up spiritual fathers.*"

Let's be the fathers God is raising up. Look for sons, develop and train them to run further than you, and I believe our leadership and ministries will be blessed beyond our wildest dreams. Just as in raising biological sons, there is risk and heartache, but we must not shrink back from this wonderful assignment.

Leadership in the Church is a challenge. Statistically, only a low percentage of us will make it through our whole lives in ministry and finish well. Let's make sure we're among those who finish well. Listen to the Holy Spirit, listen to your wife or husband, heed those leaders around you who you love and trust, and above all – have fun!

CHAPTER 6

Living in the Glory by Grace

by Joshua Mills

Several years ago, after I had finished preaching a message about the glory of God, a woman approached me with great trembling in her voice. She was experiencing something in her life that was of significant concern to her and she wanted to discuss this private matter with me. Immediately my mind began to wander; what could be so troubling to this lady? She seemed awfully shaken up. As we went into the pastor's office, she described to me some really unusual supernatural phenomena.

She began telling me about the appearance of brilliantly formed rainbows inside her home. She said they first appeared in her living room, and initially she thought they must have been a refraction of light coming through one of the windows. But later on that day as she closed the curtains and shut the blinds, these rainbows continued to shine. She said it startled her so much, that she turned off all the lights in the living room, but still the rainbows continued to brilliantly appear on the wall. She wasn't quite sure what to do. Several days later, as she was walking through her home, she noticed a rainbow shining brightly above the door to her kitchen. She was beginning to get worried that these rainbows may be coming from an ungodly source. A few days later, as she was going to set the table for dinner, she was shocked to see a rainbow appear in the middle of her dining room table!

In great despair, she told me that she could no longer invite guests over for dinner because these rainbows were appearing all over her house! I knew that this lady was sincere in her love for the Lord, and I could sense the glory in her testimony, even though she had not discerned it herself. I began sharing with her some testimonies of what we had experienced in our own lives as these supernatural rainbows miraculously appeared.

I can clearly remember the time that I was filming a television program with my good friend, Patricia King. As we were discussing the glory realm and sharing testimonies with each other, two rainbows appeared on the floor, intersecting each other in the form of a cross. This reminded us of God's promises and how Jesus Christ gave His life on Calvary so that we could enter into the promised hope of salvation. It was such a beautiful moment.

A few years later, my wife, Janet Angela, and I were ministering in Surfer's Paradise in the Gold Coast, Australia, with pastors Nuno and Amanda Marques. In each of those meetings the cloud of glory could be sensed with great intensity; words of knowledge came with ease, healing miracles were happening spontaneously and signs and wonders were flowing in a tremendous way. For almost the entire week, a rainbow appeared in our hotel room on the corner of the floor. It was amazing! Even late into the night, after we had turned off the lights in the room, this rainbow continued to brilliantly shine on the floor. I was so amazed by this wonderful sign, that I took several pictures of it with my camera. This rainbow remained in the same place for days. As I was discussing this marvelous sign with a fellow conference speaker, he told me that he had been experiencing these supernatural rainbows in his room as well!

These are just a few signs that we have seen in the glory, I think it's wonderful! In the glory you will see things you have never seen anywhere else. Jesus Christ Himself declared that "*with God all things are possible*" (Matthew 19:26). The glory realm is the dimension where the impossibilities of the earth are exchanged for the possibilities of Heaven! It is the realm where God makes a miracle out of your life! But maybe you're asking yourself, "What is the glory of God?"

Some say, that it is an otherworldly form or a divine energy force that floats in the atmosphere – something spooky or mystical. But I want to tell you that the glory of God goes beyond these things. The glory of God is His character and His divine nature, the very essence of His presence.

> "The Son is the radiance of God's glory and the exact representation of his being, sustaining all things by his powerful word."
>
> - Hebrews 1:3

He is the glory! And when God's glory touches us, the true, weighty presence of God is being released into our lives!

Throughout the Scriptures we read about the glory of God coming unto the people and visiting them in diverse manifestations. The Lord has always chosen to release His glory through unusual signs and wonders. God has always displayed Himself in remarkable ways…

The glory may come as thunder and lightning, or a very loud trumpet blast (Exodus 19:9,16). Sometimes the glory comes as a cloud (2 Chronicles 5:13-14; Exodus 40:36), sometimes it comes as fire (Exodus 40:38; Acts 2:3). Sometimes the glory comes as dew upon our clothes (Judges 6:37-38), or as a mighty rushing wind (Acts 2:2). Sometimes the glory comes as manna or heavenly provision from above (Exodus 16).

The pages of Scripture are filled with miraculous accounts of the glory of God appearing for His children, angelic encounters (1 Kings 19:5-7; Acts 10:3; Acts 12:7-11), miracles like a swirling pool of healing water (John 5:1-15), water transformed into wine (John 2:1-11), and even financial miracles released in unexpected ways (Matthew 17:27).

Why would we expect anything different today? The Bible proclaims, "Jesus Christ is the same yesterday, today and forever!" (Hebrews 13:8). The glory of God is full of miraculous signs and wonders, because it is the manifestation of a miraculous God! The glory of God always draws us closer to Him because it reveals who He is!

Often, when the glory of God comes upon me I will be filled with great joy. I think this should be commonplace among believers, as the Bible says,

"*In the presence of the Lord there is fullness of joy*" (Psalm 16:11). Unspeakable joy comes in the glory realm because in that place you realize that God's grace is available for you without labor or toil. His unmerited favor is overflowing in order to enable you to rise to higher heights.

7 TRUTHS ABOUT THE GLORY OF GOD

1. You Cannot Work Hard Enough to Earn God's Glory

In the glory we recognize that it's not our effort that bring us into this place of divine favor. We are surrounded by the greatness of His presence and we recognize how majestic He truly is! Because of Him we have access to enter into this sphere of divine blessing.

> "So let us come boldly to the throne of our gracious God. There we will receive his mercy, and we will find grace to help us when we need it most."
>
> - Hebrews 4:16 (KJV)

2. The Latter Glory Is Greater than the Former Glory

I've heard many people singing songs about desiring to see the glory of God in the same way that Moses experienced the glory, but I am bewildered by such a statement! The Scriptures clearly tell us that the glory Moses experienced was a fading glory, while the glory we can experience through Christ Jesus is an ever-increasing glory! The glory that we have access to is *greater* than the glory of former days (Haggai 2:9)! While Moses' experiences with God were amazing, he was limited to occasional visitations and miracles. Through Christ we have a continual realm of glory living on the inside of us! We have constant access to the flow of blessing and miracles! Moses' face shone after his grandiose encounter on the mountain top, but you and I can carry the radiance of God's presence on our lives each and every day!

> "And we, who with unveiled faces all reflect the Lord's glory, are being transformed into his likeness with ever-increasing glory, which comes from the Lord, who is the Spirit."
>
> - 2 Corinthians 3:18 (NIV)

3. God's Glory May Appear in a Visible Way

At times in the glory, I have seen tiny sparkles appearing in the air, or falling down upon people. Sometimes the glory will come as a shower of golden rain and sometimes this golden substance will even come out of the pores of my skin. I have seen this happen in many churches on many different people. The Bible speaks about the *shekinah* glory of God. The word *shekinah* means, "to be seen" or, "a visible manifestation of the divine presence". This supernatural golden substance is a sign of the glory of God coming upon His people. Gold represents the glory of God. In the Old Testament, the children of Israel brought their riches of gold, silver, and jewels into the wilderness tabernacle. The tabernacle was filled with these symbols of the glory of God. When the Lord gave instruction for Solomon's temple, He told them to overlay everything with gold, including the walls and ceiling! Even the veil that separated the manifest glory of God from the rest of the temple had golden thread woven into it! God has always chosen to represent His glory with a golden substance. Isn't it amazing to realize that as New Testament believers we are now the carriers of God's glory? We carry His presence here on Earth! We are His temples! If the glory of the Old Testament was just a fading glory (2 Corinthians 3:7-11), then how much more does the Lord want to cover us in the presence of His glory today!

Sometimes, as I stand in the glory, my hands and feet will begin to

drip with supernatural oil, representing the miracle anointing of God. Many times I will use this supernatural oil to pray for the sick and I've seen tremendous healing miracles take place. The supernatural oil that flows from my hands often carries a heavenly rose fragrance – the aroma of Jesus! (Song of Songs 2:1) While we were recently hosting a *School of the Supernatural* in Ottawa, Canada, one of the associate pastors approached me on the platform to show me the palms of his hands that were pooled full with supernatural fragrant oil. This oil continued to flow the entire night, and I had him lay his hands on the sick. The next morning we received a message from the church, telling us that this same miracle was happening once again as they were gathered together in worship. In Psalm 23:5, David says, "*You've anointed my head with fresh oil.*" God is anointing us with a fresh new wave of His Spirit! I believe that these things we are experiencing are simply prophetic signs of the glory of God being released upon the earth. God wants us to display His glory in the earth!

4. God's Glory May be Experienced in a Tangible Way

The Hebrew word for this glory of God is *chabod*, and it literally means, "The abundant riches, glory, splendor, and honor of God." The root word it comes from indicates a literal weight. So we see that the glory of God is a tangible presence of weighty, abundant riches, honor, and glory! Moses experienced the glory and witnessed this tangible presence.

> "[9] The Lord said to Moses, 'I am going to come to you in a dense cloud, so that the people will hear me speaking with you and will always put their trust in you.' …[16] On the morning of the third day there was thunder and lightning, with a thick cloud over the mountain, and a very loud trumpet blast."
>
> – Exodus 19:9,16 (NIV)

5. If You Embrace God's Grace You Will See His Glory

The only way to truly experience God's glory is by embracing His grace that flows freely without effort or cost. Your faith connecting with God's grace becomes the catalyst for a never-ending river of blessing to flow. Focusing on Him enables you to see His greatness in your own life.

> "But we see Jesus, who was made a little lower than the angels, now crowned with glory and honor because he suffered death, so that by the grace of God he might taste death for everyone"
>
> \- Hebrews 2:9 (NIV)

6. You Must Respond to the Glory in Order to Partake of It

I have discovered that it is absolutely essential to respond to the realm of glory. The glory realm is the atmosphere of revelatory knowledge. When you touch God's presence, He will always give you unusual instructions. God told Moses to stretch out his rod in order to see the most extraordinary signs and wonders! The Lord spoke to Joshua and told him to march around the walls of Jericho with a specific instruction detailing the exact number of times and details for victory. The blind man received his sight as he washed his eyes in the pool of Siloam according to the instructions that were given to him by Jesus Christ (John 9:7). *Whatever is revealed in the heavens becomes prophetic to the earth.*

These unusual instructions will always require unusual obedience. When responding to the realm of glory, you must be obedient to the vision that God gives.

> "[22] Do not merely listen to the word, and so deceive yourselves. Do what it says. [23] Anyone who listens to the word but does not do what it says is like a man who looks at his face in a mirror [24] and, after

> looking at himself, goes away and immediately forgets what he looks like. [25] But the man who looks intently into the perfect law that gives freedom, and continues to do this, not forgetting what he has heard, but doing it—he will be blessed in what he does."
>
> - James 1:22-25 (NIV)

Revelation demands activation in order to produce a manifestation!

Several years ago I heard a testimony about a man who had been reading the scripture passage where Elijah was supernaturally provided for by the ravens (1 Kings 17:4-6). As the man focused on this scripture he felt God instruct him to go outside and begin commanding the birds around his home to go out and bring him money! This man would go outside his house and loudly shout, "People lose money every day, so go and get it now!" Surprisingly, many birds began to gather around and they actually listened to him! Over the following days, this man found money scattered all over his back yard. Later on, a young boy was so excited by this testimony that he decided that if it had worked for this gentleman and if it had worked for Elijah, it could certainly work for him too! This boy prayed and asked the Lord to provide some money for him to sow into missionary work. After his prayer, he went outside and commanded the birds to go and gather money and to put it in a tree! On the first day this young boy found $1.65 in the tree, on the second day he discovered $2.35, and on the third day he was amazed to find a whopping $7.00! Each day as he would command the birds to go and get his money, they would listen to his instruction and put it in the tree. Over the next two months he found a grand total of $440.00 in that tree! Praise God!

It's absolutely essential that when we receive an instruction from God, that we will act in obedience to it. Sometimes these instructions will come in the form of a prophetic word, other times it will be a *rhema* word highlighted to you within the Scriptures. There are times when you will feel a specific impression upon hearing somebody else's testimony. Your obedience may require you to do something that you've never done before, but remember, *an unusual instruction will always require unusual obedience!* When the poor widow woman obeyed the instructions given to her by the prophet Elijah, it caused the floodgates of prosperity to open over her life (1 Kings 17:7-16). When the ten lepers travelled according to Jesus' instruction, they discovered divine healing for their bodies, as they were all instantly cleansed from the diseased condition (Luke 17:11-14).

Once we receive the instruction and respond to it in obedience, we must remain in faith. *Fear never produces the miraculous, but faith always does!* God's answer to our problem is often different from the solutions we've already thought of. Your faith connecting with God's grace will allow the glory realm to manifest for you in remarkable ways! Always remain in faith, believing that God's promises to you are true.

Several years ago my wife, Janet Angela was experiencing sickness that just refused to dissipate. Even after anointed prayers and continual confession of God's healing Word, this stubborn illness of congestion in her chest, and other seasonal symptoms, only appeared to increase. One morning as I was preparing for the day ahead, I heard the voice of the Lord speaking clearly to me with His divine instructions. The Holy Spirit instructed me to lay my hands on a bottle of water and ask Janet Angela to drink it for her complete healing. In the natural, it seemed like a very unusual, possibly even pointless, thing to do. But I have learned that when God speaks to me it is always for my benefit. *God is continually speaking words of blessing and favor over your life.* But you must be willing to receive that revelation in order to demonstrate that manifestation. Immediately upon hearing those divine instructions from the Lord, I proceeded towards an unopened bottle of water that was sitting on the night stand beside the bed. I had only moved a few steps towards the bottle when I began to witness the most unusual thing – what looked like a tiny tornado began to swirl on the inside of that bottle! I had not even laid my hands on the bottle yet, but suddenly, the water began to change its appearance into a deep reddish color. My son, Lincoln, and I were transfixed as we watched this awesome miracle taking place in front of our eyes. Simply moving towards the miracle in faith caused the manifestation to transpire (something similar happened for the ten lepers in Luke 17).

7. Receive God's Grace that Provides His Blessings

When we believe in the reality of God's grace, His favor that flows from the finished work of Christ on Calvary, we position ourselves to receive the greatest miracles we have ever known. A wise mentor once told me, *"God's only pain is to be doubted, His only pleasure is to be believed."* Living in the glory realm is not about a set list of religious do's and don'ts. It's simply about living a life that believes in the power and presence of God that has already set the captives free. You must believe your sin has been forgiven. You must believe your debts have been relieved. You must believe that you are healed. You must believe God.

God believes in you. He sees His promises inside of you. He believes that you can be everything He ever dreamed you could be. In the glory realm, this reality begins to manifest on the earth.

Janet Angela received that unopened bottle of water that had changed into a heavenly medicine, and as she drank that supernaturally charged water, she began to feel a fizzing inside of her body (she compared it to a gentle cleansing), and instantly every sickness disappeared. Later on, she discovered that God had brought healing to her body in many more ways than she even realized at the time. This was truly a remarkable manifestation of God's love flowing from the realms of Glory.

You can live in this realm, *you* can experience miracles in your life, *you* can receive a touch from God, because His grace is sufficient for you.

CHAPTER 7

Dealing with the Demonic

by Cornel Marais

In the past I didn't care much for the demonic. All I knew was that Jesus dealt with demons in the Bible. That all changed one day when a lady walked straight up to my brother-in-law while he was preaching and said, in a very deep and disturbing voice, "Shut up! You are preaching lies! Just shut up!" My brother-in-law angrily told the demon in the woman to be quiet and sit quietly in a chair until he was finished speaking. The demon sat down for about 5 minutes before it threw the lady to the floor and it started convulsing, screaming and cursing Jesus. When I looked around, the whole church had cleared out and the people were staring in through the doors and windows! I seriously wanted to join them, but my brother-in-law called me over and together we cast a couple of hundred demons out of this lady. My world was rocked to its core. So if you, like me, didn't care much for dealing with the demonic, what you are about to read might come as a shock to you too. However, I also know what you are about to read will enable you to administer freedom in a whole new dimension!

Do We Even Need to Deal with the Demonic?

For many people, dealing with the demonic means to stand around in circles attacking regional and other demons until a perceived breakthrough happens. They call that 'spiritual warfare'. You won't find anything in Scripture to support that. Neither Jesus nor Paul ever did anything like it either. Demons feed off people, so if you want to see change in your community, change the people in your community. Real warfare is waged by getting people out from under demonic control. For one kingdom to advance, another has to retreat. Dealing with the demonic the way Jesus did, means casting actual demons out of actual people. Before Jesus left, He gave us final instructions, one of which was to cast out demons (Mark 16:17). So yes, you need to deal with the demonic and you are 100 times more likely to encounter them in people than anywhere else.

Jesus' ministry was categorized by mainly three activities: He taught, He healed, and He cast out demons. If we are to imitate Christ and do the same and greater works that He did, we are going to have to start casting out demons too. For some reason, deliverance is probably the most neglected ministry in the body today. Whether that is because of stigma, shame, fear, lack of knowledge or simply living in denial, I don't know. All I know is that over the years I have encountered thousands of demons in just as many people.

James taught us to "resist the devil and he will flee from you" (James 4:7). That means he is going to come after you at some point and you are going to have to resist him to make him stop. Peter tells us, in 1 Peter 5:8, that we are to be vigilant, because the devil is looking for somebody to devour. Be vigilant, on guard, attentive, on the alert. The Greek word used in that verse for vigilant is *gregoreuo* and it means, "To take heed lest through remission (decrease in action) and indolence (laziness, inactivity, apathy) some form of destruction comes upon you and overtakes you." The only way to ensure defeat is to stop fighting. Paul tells us in Romans 16:20, that God will crush satan under your feet. That is not some sort of prophetic action, it is actually casting him out and destroying his works (1 John 3:8). If you don't step on him, he is not being crushed. If you don't resist him, he is not going to flee. If you don't cast him out, he is going to stay around. You have been given both power and authority to deal with the demonic. Shrugging it off as superstitious nonsense because of a theology based in fear, denial, and shame, is exactly what the devil wants you to do. Paul teaches in 2 Corinthians 2:11, that being ignorant of the devil's schemes and devices gives him an advantage over us. So by learning about him, how to destroy his works, and cast him out of people, you are taking back your advantage.

Please note, I am not trying to condemn you for not fighting, I am try-

ing to empower you to actually be more effective. When you wake up in the morning, Hell should go on high alert! James teaches us that demons tremble because they believe there is one God (James 2:19). God literally lives in you with the fullness of His power and authority, and demons tremble when you step into a room. Jesus told us that we have the keys of the kingdom and that the gates of Hell will not prevail against us. That's right, us; you and me. If you have ever watched an epic adventure movie like the Lord of the Rings, you will have seen people inside a gated city defending an onslaught from outside. Gates are defensive structures. If the gates of Hell will not prevail, it means the devil and Hell are supposed to be in defense mode against our onslaught. Think about it, are you the one always defending against the devil's onslaught or is he defending against you? If you are doing all the defending, you are already on the back foot. The best defense is a better offense. It is time to take back your advantage and start going after the gates! The devil has one purpose, and that is to be defeated by you!

How Do I Know if I Have a Demon?

There are two ways to check for demons in a person: discernment and detection. Discernment is when the Holy Spirit reveals the presence of a demon in a person through the gift of discernment of spirits (1 Corinthians 12:10; Acts 16:16-17). Sometimes I will meet a person for ministry and I just know that I know their problem is demonic. Detection is simply observing what demons are up to in a person's life, which is usually more obvious to others than to the affected person (Matthew 15:22). Demons don't go around like big monsters trying to hurt people, they work covertly. Chances are, that if you have one, you're not even aware of it. Or you are aware of a problem, you just don't know it might be a demon.

> "When Jesus saw that the people came running together, He rebuked the unclean spirit, saying to it: 'Deaf and dumb spirit, I command you, come out of him and enter him no more!"
>
> - Mark 9:25 (NKJV)

This guy was deaf and dumb as a result of a demon in him. After Jesus addressed the demon directly and commanded it to get out, it left, and the man was well again. Is all deafness and dumbness caused by demons? Of course not. You get natural sickness and demonic sickness. But it really doesn't matter which you have, you deal with both natural and demonic sickness in the same way: with authority and faith. Address it directly, command it to go and don't take no for an answer. Demons also have names, usually associated with their function. The deaf and dumb spirit causes deaf and dumbness. The spirit of fear causes fear, etc. A spirit of infirmity causes sickness. If you know the name, use it. If you don't, just be general.

The five main areas where we have found demons operating most often in and through people are:

1. **Various physical infirmities** – Luke 13:11; Mark 9:25; Matthew 9:32; Matthew 17:15.
2. **Various mental & emotional problems** – Mark 5:15; Luke 6:18; Acts 5:16; Matthew 15:22.
3. **Sexual problems & addictions** – No specific scripture, just common sense and experience.
4. **Occultic practices and religious error** – Mark 1:23-25; Acts 19:19; Isaiah 47:12-14; Acts 16:16; Gal 3:1. This category also includes involvement in other religions, superstitious- and occultic practices like witchcraft or divination, as well as having objects and paraphernalia associated with the occult or other religions in your home (Deuteronomy 7:25-26). Whenever we have worked

with Hindus, Satanists or other religions, the gods and idols they worshipped manifested in them as demons.

5. **Relationships** – This is probably more an area demons tend to focus on than one that they operate through. Demons want to destroy your relationship with God, your spouse, siblings, parents, children, friends, etc.

But What if I am Saved? Can a Demon Still Get in Me?

I have cast too many demons out of believers to still think they can't get in, and there is no scripture that says demons can't inhabit believers. Just the fact that demons cause various kinds of sicknesses which believers and non-believers alike get, shows they have the ability to get in.

Don't confuse ability with right. The Cross took away the devil's right (Colossians 2:15), it didn't take away his ability (1 Peter 5:8). The real question should be, 'How deep can they go?' What I mean is that demons can get into your body in the form of sickness and disease. They can also get into your soul, messing with your emotions, will, thoughts, etc. In other forms like curses they can get hold of your finances, relationships, jobs, home life, etc. Demons can't, however, live in your spirit. As a believer, your spirit has become one with the Holy Spirit and you have been sealed off, meaning a believer can't be demon-possessed. There is a difference between you having/possessing a demon and a demon having/possessing you. I have witnessed demons manifest and take over the bodies and minds of many believers during deliverance sessions, controlling both their actions and speech, just as it is also recorded in the Gospels, but this kind of thing is more of a stall tactic aimed at intimidating and scaring you in the hopes that you will give up (Mark 1:23-24).

How Did They Get in Me?

The obvious answer for this, according to many preachers, would be sin. Conventional teaching on demonology proposes that sin opens a door to the devil or gives the devil a right to mess with you. I totally disagree with that. The way I see it, is that the devil *never* has a right, no matter what you did. To say he has a right or has gained a right is the same as saying a thief had a right to steal my car because I didn't lock it, or the rapist had a right to rape the woman because she wore a short dress. It's just stupid. Have you ever heard somebody in a courtroom argue that the victim deserved to have this bad thing happen to him or her because they are harboring unforgiveness? Please, if that nonsense won't stand in our natural judicial systems, why would you even think they would stand in God's?

Secondly, if the devil had a right to be there, I wouldn't have the right to cast him out, which makes Jesus' instructions to cast out demons illegitimate. That being said, please note that sin will destroy your life, with or without the devil's help. Sin will make it easier for him to get through to you and in to you undetected, but it will never give him a right to be there.

So how do they get in? Simple answer: Illegally. The exact details of how they got in, when and why is not a prerequisite for deliverance, but knowing how and when they got in can help when you disciple people on how to live free, after you have cast the demons out (2 Corinthians 2:11; Matthew 12:43-45).

How Does One Go about Doing Deliverance?

You can do deliverance on yourself, and by yourself, but I find it more effective when believers minister to one another (James 5:16). Unless the

presence of a demon is discerned, you would have to detect whether there might be a few (Yes, a few, they seldom work alone). Look at the categories I listed above and make a thorough list of suspect and problem areas in your life. Be honest, and ask the Holy Spirit for discernment too.

Once you have your list, do what Jesus did. Address the problem as though it were a demon and command it to go in Jesus' name. Once you have commanded it to leave, do a quick body check for anything 'manifesting'. For example, when we address a spirit of witchcraft the persons will often report a manifestation in their hands or fingers (Micah 5:12). Manifestations range from almost nothing happening to very violent and severe. These manifestations serve one purpose: To get the person ministering to stop through fear and intimidation. Common manifestations include: bubbling or uneasiness in the stomach, nausea, coughing, a choking feeling in the throat, restrictive sensation or tightness over the chest and throat, screaming, yelling, sudden headache the moment you start praying, cursing, falling and shaking, tingling, pain, discomforts, disorientation, cloudy thoughts, inability to speak, and the sensation of something moving inside the person's body.

We have seen many diverse manifestations while doing deliverance, including people acting like animals, especially slithering like snakes with their tongues darting in and out while making hissing sounds. We have had demons speak through the people, just like they did in the Bible, and then they often give the person unnatural strength (Acts 19:14-16). I'm not saying this to make it sensational, but to bring attention back to a neglected area of ministry, to show you the fight is real, with real demons in real people. I am also telling you so you know what to expect and what to do when you encounter the same thing.

When a manifestation happens, focus on that area and whatever spirit you just addressed. For example, if you address the spirit of witchcraft and the person's hands start to burn or tingle, lay hands on their hands and command the spirit of witchcraft to leave. Do this until the manifestation stops and peace returns to the person. If another person placed the witchcraft on them, have them pronounce a blessing over that person (Matthew 5:44). Many times people will want to scream, cough, or break wind. The word for "spirit" in the Hebrew and Greek means, "air, breath, or wind", and the expulsion of air is the demon actually leaving the person's body.

A Demon Manifested and We Got it out, Now What?

Jesus actually taught on this. Let's have a look:

> "[43] When an unclean spirit goes out of a man, he goes through dry places, seeking rest, and finds none. [44] Then he says, 'I will return to my house from which I came.' And when he comes, he finds it empty, swept, and put in order. [45] Then he goes and takes with him seven other spirits more wicked than himself, and they enter and dwell there; and the last state of that man is worse than the first. So shall it also be with this wicked generation."
>
> \- Matthew 12:43-45 (NKJV)

When demons leave they seek rest. To them, rest is where they can express their corrupt nature in and through people. That is why they return to the person out of which they were cast in order to find rest. When Jesus says it goes back to its "*house*", He is referring to the person. If the house is empty, they just go back in. What does an empty house look like? Let's say a spirit of addiction is cast out of a smoker. If they then continue the physical habit of smoking, the spirit of addiction will come back and find the house empty, unchanged (Titus 2:11-12). Both the spirit and the habit need to be dealt with.

We actually had an interesting case with a smoker once. We addressed addiction and a demon manifested, but refused to leave. We asked it why it was refusing to go and it answered us, *"Because my name is not addiction, my name is Baal. Every time she smokes it is a smoke offering to me."* Needless to say we got Baal out, but we thought that was very interesting and looked it up. We found a verse in Jeremiah 32:29 where smoke offerings were made to Baal by the Chaldeans. This is why knowing how, why and which demons came in can help. It gives us information to help disciple people. We don't disciple into freedom, we set free first and then disciple how to live free.

Where To from Here?

Firstly, don't become demon-obsessed or go out on a witch-hunt telling all your friends they have demons. Study the Gospels again and specifically look at the instances where Jesus and the disciples encountered demons. Look at what they said, how they dealt with each encounter, and what Jesus taught about the demonic. Start with your own life and begin to actively resist the devil. It is not a-say-it-once-and-everything-is-OK kind of thing either. Demons can be very stubborn, that is why they are to be cast or driven out. Our fight against them is compared to wrestling (Ephesians 6:12), a very close and intimate battle. If you are in a safe environment like a home group, you might begin by ministering to each other in the group. You will be surprised by the freedom you are able to minster when you actively start resisting the devil and casting demons out. Learn to hear the Holy Spirit's guidance during these ministry times too.

We can't cover everything about deliverance in one short chapter, it is more a case of on the job training with the Holy Spirit. Here are a few extra pointers that will help you on your way:

- Don't follow formulas or Old Covenant teachings. Most of what is out there is based in Old Covenant, law based thinking. These include the belief that demons have to be mentioned by name or that sin needs to be confessed before the demons will leave. In our experience, it is easier to deal with demons if sin has been dealt with, but dealing with sin and dealing with demons are two different ministries. Having a demon's name or function does help too, but you can cast it out without knowing its name.

- Try to never minister alone, especially when ministering to the opposite gender. Jesus also sent the disciples out in two's. This is not a rule, just a practical thing to protect everybody involved.
- Respect other people's privacy. Don't go telling the whole world that John had a spirit of lust cast out of him.
- Minister to children with their parents present. Be careful of saying words like evil spirits, demons, etc. when ministering to them. Don't get shouty and aggressive either; you will freak the kids and parents out. You don't want to scare them, you are there to help. Use 'PG' prayer…
- Don't try the stuff you see in the movies; holy water, crosses, holding up Bibles, garlic, or saying things like, "The Spirit of Christ compels you!" That doesn't do diddlysquat to help anybody.
- Don't make a spectacle or draw attention to manifestations. If they start happening, tell the demon to stop the manifestations and command them to leave. If they start talking to you, tell them to shut up and get out.
- Anointing with oil helps, as does worshipping and praying in tongues, but don't make them into formulas or traditions. Where possible, let one person do the casting out while the others help by either worshipping Jesus in the background and/or praying in tongues. Demons hate it when we worship and glorify Jesus. Just remember,

demons aren't worshipped out of people, they are cast out of them.

- Ask the Holy Spirit for help. That is why He is there. He is your Helper.
- Keep a record of what happens, and what demons you encounter with regards to specific manifestations. It will help you in the future. Respect confidentiality of course. You might quickly learn, for example, that the spirit of depression and the spirit of discouragement are usually accompanied by the spirit of suicide and the spirit of hopelessness. So the next time somebody says they feel totally hopeless, you can go after that and the other three when you attack. Most of the names will be given either by discernment to those ministering or by the person being ministered to. Pay close attention to what goes through your mind.
- Ask for constant feedback about sensations, feelings, emotions, thoughts, etc. that the person being ministered to might be experiencing.
- Remember the word for spirit is the same as air, that is why demons often leave with screams, yells, coughs, sneezes, etc. When people start coughing, the demons are leaving. (Have a bucket and tissues handy, some leave with vomiting…)
- You don't have to have a manifestation or sensation to be sure the demon left. Some leave without any manifestation whatsoever. If there is no manifestation, how do we know there even was a demon in the first place? You will know by the change in the person's life after ministry.
- Make sure people who are being ministered to always feel safe and respected. Let them know you are addressing demons, not them. Remind them that God loves them and wants to see them free.
- Demons are very stubborn. Address them like you would a naughty

dog. Be stern, be authoritative. Remember you are issuing them with commands, not suggestions. Jesus has given you His authority. The same Spirit that raised Christ from the dead lives in you!

I trust that you are now more informed about this topic, and even willing to go step on some devils, rather than being just plain shocked or offended at what you have just read. The greatest exercise I believe any believer can do to understand the authority they have been entrusted with, is to go cast out demons. I have prayed for the sick without seeing them healed, but I have never come across a demon I could not cast out. Your authority will transform from a knowledgeable concept into life-giving effectiveness. Now go crush some devils with those big grace boots you have on! God supplies the crushing power, you supply the feet! (Romans 16:20) You step, He crushes!

Grace, peace and freedom to you all!

Chapter 8

Grace and Finances

by Andrew Wommack

I know that people hate American preachers talking about money, but it is a fact of life that we have to have money to be able to live and preach the Gospel. I struggled for 30 years in the area of finances, not in any way victorious or prosperous, merely just making ends meet. There is way too much that happened for me to be able to share it all with you here, but God totally turned my life around in this area, and in the last decade our income has increased at least 20 or 30 times. We couldn't have done what we are doing today if God hadn't touched me in this area of finances. I wouldn't be here if there hadn't been an increased revelation in the area of prosperity in my life, so I just want to share a few of those truths with you.

Let me start by making it clear that the number one thing that is offensive about the prosperity message is greed! The way that it's all presented, is about how you get more of everything. That is not what God showed me about prosperity. My wife and I have lived in the same house for 22 years. We have nice cars, but they aren't fancy cars. Most of my staff have nicer homes than me. I do not use prosperity for me, but at the same time, you cannot be a blessing to anyone else if you aren't blessed. This is what the Lord told Abraham in Genesis 12:3. He said, "I will bless you and make your name great and you shall be a blessing." He had to be blessed before he could be a blessing.

I know that there will be many ministers reading this who have big things in their heart that they want to do for the Lord, and yet most are limited in how much of that vision they can achieve, because of their financial situation. That is not God's way! Let me also say that prosperity will work in any nation. This isn't just limited to the "prosperous" nations of this world. God will work miracles in your finances, just the same as He will in your body or your marriage. If you're thinking that it won't work in your country, you're wrong. I know that there's a lot of resistance against teaching prosperity, and I'm aware that many people will reject what I have to say before they even read it. But for those of you who have ears to hear, I have great things to share with you.

I want to share a parable with you that used to make no sense to me. This is a parable about a man who stole money from his master, and when the master found out about it, he said, "Put your books in order because I'm going to review them, and if what I heard is true, I'm going to fire you."

The man knew he had been stealing money from his master, so he knew he would lose his job. He continued to steal money from his master, but now instead of putting the money into his own pocket, he started to give it to other people, and he said the reason he did it was so that when he was fired, they would let him into their houses. He was using his master's money to bribe people. The logic was that when he was fired, he would simply remind them of all the money he gave them, and they would feel obligated to take care of his needs.

> "[1] He also said to His disciples: 'There was a certain rich man who had a steward, and an accusation was brought to him that this man was wasting his goods. [2] So he called him and said to him, 'What is this I hear about you? Give an account of your stewardship, for you can no longer be steward.'
>
> [3] "Then the steward said within himself, 'What shall I do? For my master is taking the stewardship away from me. I cannot dig; I am ashamed to beg. [4] I have resolved what to do, that when I am put out of the stewardship, they may receive me into their houses.'
>
> [5] "So he called every one of his master's debtors to him, and said to the first, 'How much do you owe my master?' [6] And he said, 'A hundred measures of oil.' So he said to him, 'Take your bill, and sit down quickly and write fifty.' [7] Then he said to another, 'And how

> much do you owe?' So he said, 'A hundred measures of wheat.' And he said to him, 'Take your bill, and write eighty.'"
>
> - LUKE 16:1-7 (NKJV)

Now, this entire story is not unusual up until this point, but what is really strange is the master's reaction to this in verse 8:

> "So the master commended the unjust steward because he had dealt shrewdly. For the sons of this world are more shrewd in their generation than the sons of light."

So why would the master commend his servant who stole money from him? How many of you would compliment a thief who was robbing your house? The fact that this man was so detached from his money so he could see something good in the thief is amazing, and this was one of the main reasons the man was rich! Why did he compliment this servant for stealing his money? I believe it all comes down to the fact that he had found the proper use of money.

Prior to this time, the man had been stealing all of his money, but he hadn't been saving any of it. You can prove that in verse three:

> "Then the steward said within himself, 'What shall I do? For my master is taking the stewardship away from me. I cannot dig; I am ashamed to beg."

This shows he hadn't saved any of the money, because he was going to have to dig (go to work), or beg.

Of all the money he had stolen, he hadn't taken and invested it or kept it, he had been buying flat screen TV's, cars, and MP3 players. He had blown it on temporary things, but when it looked like he was going to lose his job he was forced to think about the future, so he started to use his

money to change his future.

This is one of the great truths about money; it has power in it. Just that thought is offensive to most Christians. In the King James Bible, they even call it "*filthy lucre*" to make it sound really bad. Christians have been taught that money is evil. The Bible doesn't say money is evil; 1 Timothy 6:10 says it is the love of money that is evil. Money itself is not evil. If you believe money is evil, then send it to me. If you really believe it's evil, get rid of all of it. Money is not evil, and because of our religious preconceptions, we have turned many godly people away from the Church because they have money.

I could take $100 and use it to bless someone or to curse someone. I could give it to you and say, "God wanted me to give this to you," and you would be blessed, or I could use that same money and entice you to do something wrong. Money isn't good or bad; it's what you choose to do with it that makes it good or bad. This parable teaches that using money just for your immediate needs is wrong.

The real power in money is to affect your future. There are many scriptures that equate money to seed. 2 Corinthians 9:10 says, "*God gives seeds to sowers,*" and if you look at the context, it's talking about money. Money is like a seed. There's power in a seed, you can eat a seed and it will give you energy, but the greatest power in a seed is to plant it. When you plant a seed, it brings a hundred fold return. You can plant a little tiny seed, and it comes back a huge tree. There's power in a seed!

I have a rock on my property that is the size of a large building. It's a huge boulder. I chiseled a chair into it, and I sit out there and worship the Lord. On the top of that rock there's a little hole about the size of a softball. It traps water, and when dirt got in there, and a seed got in there, a tree started growing in the top of this rock, as it grew, it eventually split this massive boulder. That is the power that was in that tiny little seed.

Money has power in it, and yes, we have to take care of our immediate needs; it doesn't glorify God for you to live under a bridge. The Lord wants to take care of your needs, but the greatest use of money is to affect your future. This man in the parable affected his immediate future on the earth, but the point of this parable is how we can use money to affect eternity.

Money is temporary. Actually, all kinds of physical wealth; jewelry, diamonds, everything that is valuable in this life, will be worth nothing in the life to come. You could live in the nicest house, but it's eventually going to perish, everything natural is going to perish. But you can take something that is temporary and turn it into something which is eternal. You do that when you plant money into the Gospel. When you use money to touch other people's lives, its benefits will never leave you.

While speaking at a conference in Hong Kong, I met a woman who lives on an island who had first come across my teaching about eight years before. When she first heard of me, she had just been born again. She had a terrible past, and was living under great depression. She told me that she would have killed herself if she hadn't gotten hold of that teaching, and now her life is totally changed. She now has a ministry to the Filipino maids on that island, and she has seen miracles happen and people being saved, all because people took money and invested it into other's lives – this is what prosperity is all about.

It's not about having more houses and cars! How many beds do you need to sleep in? How many toilets to take care of your personal business? Sooner or later, you just ought to be satisfied with what you have.

Does that mean you quit believing God because your needs are met? I have people criticizing me and saying, "You're just preaching that people can have more things." They tell me that God's been good to them,

they've been blessed and they won't ask God for any more. They say that believing God for prosperity is selfish. What I'm saying is that if you have all you need and if you're satisfied and don't want any more, *that's* selfish. You think money is just for you, so once your needs are met; forget the rest of the world. You're making the same mistake the servant made. You're taking all the prosperity that God has given you, to just buy things here on earth. But the real power in money is to touch other people's lives. The real power of money is released when you give it to touch someone else.

We have to change this selfish and short term mentality – this is why the Lord gave this parable. He interprets the parable in verse 9, and here is what Jesus said:

> "And I say to you, make friends for yourselves by unrighteous mammon, that when you fail, they may receive you into an everlasting home."

What this literally means, is, use money to touch people's lives so that when you die they will receive something that will never perish. Take something that's going to perish, and turn it into something that's never going to perish. You can take money and turn it into a changed life.

I can promise you this, that when we get to Heaven, not one of you is going to come up to me and say, "I wish you had never encouraged me to give away so much money into the Gospel." There's not going to be one person who says, "I wish I had bought a new TV or a new car instead." All that stuff is going to be gone! Everything you buy in this life stays here and is destroyed, but everything you give away to touch people's lives goes into eternity.

So we have a choice. Are we just going to use money and let it be destroyed forever, or are we going to let it be turned into something that's eternal? If we really understood this, we would completely change our whole outlook: Instead of trying to see how much we could *get,* we would see how much we could *fund.*

In North America we say, "You get all you can, you can all you get, then you sit on your can." That's the wrong attitude! What we should do, is see how much we can possibly give away. Last year, my wife and I were blessed to be able to give away 80% of what we got. I don't believe in prosperity so that I can have more things, I believe in prosperity so that I can make a difference in this world. I've learned the real power in money. I'm using it to change people's lives all over the world. I've also come to realize that it's a blessing to get other people to give.

In 1 Kings 17, there's a great example of this. Elisha was sent to a city to save a woman who was dying of starvation. This woman was down to her last little bit of food; all she had was enough to prepare one last meal for her and her son. Elisha came to her and said, "Feed me first."

Get this picture; here's a preacher asking a woman to give her last little bit of food to him (He had to be American, he was going to take the last bite out of a widow's mouth). This would have made headlines all over the world, "PREACHER TAKES WIDOW'S LAST MEAL".

What people don't realize, is that he wasn't taking *from* her, he was giving *to* her. She only had enough for one meal. Instead of wasting that and eating it, Elisha told her to plant it as a seed. If what you have isn't enough for your need, use it as seed and plant it. Some people think that when you give, the money is leaving your life. That would be true if there wasn't a God who sees it as seed that He will multiply back to you. God did say that when you give, it would be given back to you. It's not losing, it's receiving.

This is a matter of faith. People who don't have faith will always see giving as losing money, but if you can believe the promises of God, that seed never leaves your life, it just enters into your future where it grows, multiplies, and comes back to you. We have the promise that it will come back in this life one hundred fold, and in the life to come. It will come back forever in the people's lives you've changed. It's not foolish to take something that is going to perish and turn it into something that will never perish. It's not foolish to take something you cannot keep and turn it into something you cannot lose. If you understand the real potential and power of money, you will look at every dollar you get as a potential seed, and that will totally change your life.

> "He who is faithful in what is least is faithful also in much; and he who is unjust in what is least is unjust also in much."
>
> - Luke 16:10 (KJV)

This verse is often taken out of context. We tell people, "If you cannot lead a Bible study then you cannot pastor a church. If you won't clean the toilets, you won't be trusted with something greater in church." Those are true statements; this principle applies in more than one way; you do have to be faithful in small things before you're counted worthy to do greater things, but the context of this is money. Jesus is saying that trusting Him in this area of money is the *least* use of your faith. If you don't exercise your faith to become faithful in this area you cannot succeed in any area.

This is exactly the opposite of the way the body of Christ looks at this. People think that talking about money is for the "super saints", the "professional Christians". I've had people criticize me and say, "How dare you spend money on television and talk about finances, you ought to just stick to preaching the Gospel." But if you study the Gospels, Jesus talked more about money than He did about Heaven and Hell.

In Mark 10, He talked to a rich young ruler, and even though this man was very demonstrative and threw himself at Jesus, the Lord knew his heart wasn't right. This man called Jesus a good master, but Jesus said, "Why are you calling me good? There's only one good and that's God." To paraphrase, "Either call me God, or quit calling me good," and the man responded by just saying "master". He dropped the good. He wasn't willing to call Jesus God, he wasn't willing to make a real commitment to Jesus as the only way to the Father. How did Jesus reveal this lack of commitment in his heart? He used money. He told this man to sell everything he had and give it to the poor, but He didn't tell anyone else that. Zaccheus was a very wealthy man, but Jesus didn't tell him to sell everything. You don't have to give away everything you own to be a Christian, but you do have to make Jesus your Lord, and this man was not willing to do that. Jesus used money to reveal where his loyalty lay.

If we applied that same standard today, there would be a lot less people claiming to be Christians. It's easy to say, "Jesus is my Lord," but how do we know if that is really a heart-felt commitment? According to what Jesus says, money is the least expression of our faith. If you cannot do that which is least, you cannot do that which is greatest. Yet I meet people all the time who say, "Jesus is my Lord," and yet they cannot trust the promise that if you give, it will be given back to you. They say, "Well I want to give, and I would give, if I had anything extra." They're really saying that they don't believe they're going to get it back. If they really believed the Scriptures, that if you give, it will come back to you; good measure, pressed down, shaken together, and running over, then they would give.

If I told you that for every person that gives $100 to me, I'd give them back $1,000 and you knew I had the ability to fulfill that promise, you'd be absolutely stupid to not give me $100. If you didn't have it, you'd borrow it. If you really believed that I would do it, you'd give.

God has promised us exactly that, and the only reason why people don't give according to His instructions, is because they do not believe that His promise is true. You can protest all you want, but that's the bottom line.

Some of you will say, "I'm not very strong in that area, but I'm strong in believing for healing, and I can prophesy. I can do the great things, but I can't do the little things." You're deceiving yourselves. I know thousands and thousands of Christians, but I don't know one Christian that I consider to be mature, who does not have this revelation on giving. That's because you cannot be mature without trusting God in that which is least. On the other hand, I know thousands of immature Christians, and time and again they do not consistently trust God in their finances. They may give when they have some extra so that if it doesn't work they don't miss anything, but if their finances are tight they'll quit giving. Those people are immature Christians.

You have to start doing the least things before you can build yourself up to do the bigger things. You have to lift 5 pounds before you can lift 100 pounds. I meet Christians all the time who say, "I'm trusting God for my eternal salvation, but I cannot trust God for something little and insignificant like money."

I know many of you may take this as criticism, but it's not meant that way. I'm trying to help you! I remember ministering this message about 15 years ago, and after I got through, it I felt like I needed to receive an offering. I had stirred up people's faith, and they needed an opportunity to act, so I received an offering and gave it to the pastor so that no one would think that I had preached it for selfish reasons. Afterwards, the Lord spoke to me and said, "Watch what happens because these people have started trusting me in this little thing." Two totally deaf people, who had never heard, had their ears opened. People came out of wheelchairs, miracles started happening all over the congregation, and we had people run to the front, begging me to let them get saved. I didn't even give an invitation for salvation. They just saw the power of God in demonstration and it all happened when people started trusting him in this area of finances.

It is imperative that the body of Christ understands that it is not because you haven't given that God doesn't heal or bless you, but it's just the principle. If you cannot lift 5 pounds, you definitely cannot lift 100 pounds. If your faith is not capable of being exercised for the smallest things, it's not qualified for the bigger things.

God gave you seed – money. Some of it is for eating, and some of it you plant. If you don't plant, you will never reap. It's just a law of God. Your faith needs to be strong, and it starts by trusting Him in the area of finances.

I have changed my attitude, and I realize there is no shortage of money. Everyone has money. You might think that you don't have enough, but it's just a matter of priorities. If all you have is a dollar, then you have a few cents you can give. God doesn't look at the size of the gift; He deals in percentages. A person who has a dollar and gives ten cents, gives a bigger gift than a millionaire who gives one thousand dollars. Every person has something they can give, and if you give fifty cents out of a dollar you have given a huge gift, and it starts releasing the huge power of God. God isn't responding to your giving, your giving is a response to God.

I find this really simple, and yet some people have only seen it one way. They think that I'm saying that if they do this, then God has to do that. No! God has already done His part, and He gave it to you in seed form. He doesn't give you the full tree; He gives you the seed that will produce the tree. You have a choice; are you going to eat it, or sow it? Eat enough so you'll be healthy to sow and reap, but take as much as you can, and start planting it. When you do that, the supernatural power that's in the seed begins to grow, and as the Lord supplies for other people, He'll also meet your need.

My wife and I have gone through extreme poverty. We live in the

United States, where there's no reason for us to live in poverty. But when I started in the ministry we nearly starved to death. We were eligible for food stamps (welfare), but I wouldn't do it. I was trusting God the best I knew. Once, when my wife was eight months pregnant, we went two weeks without food. We came close to dying the first five to six years that I was in ministry. We were poor, and yet when I began to see these truths about giving, I started giving.

Once, we needed a new car (the car I was driving was really bad), yet we decided to buy cars for other people. Other people would go buy a car and get a loan and I would pay their loan, while I was driving a car that was really bad. I didn't do that so I could get something, but I've had over 12 cars given to me! They were nice cars, they were embarrassing cars! People would think a preacher shouldn't drive a car that nice, but they were a gift. What do I do, turn it down because I'm worried about what people think, and then buy one that costs me money? That's stupid! I've given away a dozen cars, and I've been given a dozen cars. I don't give to get, but I give knowing that I'm going to get, so I can be a bigger giver.

Since I've learned this truth, I count it a privilege to receive every penny from people that I possibly can. If I don't encourage you to give, you're going to blow it on things. You're going to get your fifth flat screen TV, and then one day you're going to stand at the gates of Heaven and nobody's going to be there to greet you. You'll be so sorry that you wasted all those seeds on temporary things. I can promise you this, when we get to Heaven, you're going to kiss me and thank me and hug me for getting that money out of your pocket, because it's only what you give away that you get to keep. Money is not that important. It's necessary, it's a tool, but it's what money can do for your future that's really powerful.

I preached this same message in Texas one time, and there was a woman who came forward for prayer, and she asked me, "You don't recognize

me, do you?"

I said, "I don't think I've ever seen you before."

She replied, "When I came to your meeting here in this church last year, I was in a mental institution. They only let me out on the weekends so I could go to church. You prayed over me that God would restore my mind and that I would be released, and the very next week they let me out of that mental institution."

This woman was so changed, I didn't even recognize her. She was working as a janitor in that mental institution, and they gave her a room to sleep in, so even though she was no longer a patient, she was still living there. She said, "I want to get away from those crazy people."

She asked me to pray that she would get a new job and a new place to live. I had just finished preaching this message about Elisha and the widow of Zarephath giving him her last bit of food. So I said to her, "What do you have to give?"

She went back and got her purse and came forward. She had $86.23. She said that was all the money she had until her next paycheck.

"I haven't even bought groceries yet, it's all I have."

I said, "Give it to me!"

She decided to give me every bit of that money. I gave it to the pastor so no one would think that I had done it for my benefit. Then I prayed over the seed that she sowed for a miracle.

God didn't respond to her actions and give her a miracle. This is where people get offended about prosperity. They think your giving is making God move, like putting money in a machine, pulling a handle and making

God come out. No. God has already provided your miracle, but it's in seed form and you have to have faith to plant it.

This woman stopped eating all her seed and decided to plant some instead. The pastor of that church called me the next week. He told me that on Monday, a man gave her a car. She didn't even ask for a car. This man hadn't been at church then, so he didn't know what had happened the day before. God just supernaturally gave her a car. On Wednesday, her mother called her. She hadn't talked to her mother in years. Her mother was embarrassed over her daughter's mental state, but out of the blue her mother just called. She found out her daughter had been set free from her mental problems, and became ashamed of the way she had treated her daughter. She asked her daughter to forgive her and to move back home. That lady got her new place to live, and by Friday she had a brand new job in a new place that paid her twice as much money.

Now God didn't do that in response to what she did. Faith is just our positive response to what God has already done by grace. God had already commanded the blessing upon her, just like He has for every person who is born-again. God has commanded His power to supply every need that you have, but He doesn't just rain the money out of Heaven. Deuteronomy 8:18 says:

> "...He who gives you power to get wealth..."

He does not give you wealth; He gives you the power to get wealth. That power is faith. Money is the seed, and when you plant that seed in faith, that's how prosperity comes. This woman didn't make God move, God had already moved. He gave her seed, but she was eating all her seed, instead of planting it.

When you plant your seed in faith, it releases the supernatural power of God. Once you understand this, it changes the way you talk about finances.

You're no longer apologetic for encouraging people to give.

It has now been decades since I have ever prayed and asked God for any money. I never ask God to bless me. I never pray for finances. My faith is worth more than just using it over money. I use my faith to relate to God, and yet I must have over $2,000,000 every month just to pay my bills. Money flows through me. I give away lots and lots of money. I have giving accounts that are just full of money and I'm looking for people to give to.

Some of you say, "Look no further!" You still haven't understood! You just want to prosper so you can have more, and I will not reward that by giving to you. The people I give to understand the principle of giving, I give seed to people who are sowers, not people who are eaters.

Because the Bible says faith without works is dead, look for an opportunity to sow. Don't think that your giving is going to make God do something, but believe that God, by grace, has already commanded His blessing on you, and that the money you have is part of His blessing. If you would look at this money as seed and mix it with faith, it would start releasing the power that's in that money to change your future.

Take the opportunity to plant a seed. It doesn't have to be a big seed, just take a moment when you're finished reading this chapter, and find a place, your local church, for example, to plant a seed into, and sow that seed into the Kingdom of God.

Let me ask you a couple of questions first.

- Did you understand the power that's in money before reading this chapter?
- Did you only give when it is convenient but you aren't committed to giving?

If that's you, we're going to pray a prayer that will change this attitude in you, and if you will respond to this prayer in faith, your life is going to change. If God can get the money through you, He'll get it to you, but if you build a dam and store it all up, it hinders the flow. You have to remain a river and never become a lake. The eyes of the Lord search the earth, looking for somebody with a pure heart in this area, and if you will become faithful in this which is least, then God will start doing even greater things through you.

> Father I pray for all those who are reading this right now. They have admitted they have only given when it is convenient, and we change that mindset right now. We repent of not understanding these simple truths, and we make a commitment that we are going to start trusting You in our finances. We believe that this is the least use of our faith, and as we trust You in that which is least, we will be emboldened to trust You in that which is greater. We make that commitment before You and we stand on the promise that You keep that which we commit. Father we believe You are going to bring us back to this commitment that You will help us to keep it, that You will encourage us, even in the time of waiting for the harvest, and I thank You in advance for the miracles that You will release. Thank You for the people that will now be able to preach the Gospel without worry. Thank You for the millions of lives that will be changed because of this. We give You the praise for that in Jesus name, Amen.

CHAPTER 9

Titus: Stress These Things

The Place of Grace in Balanced Preaching

by Chad M. Mansbridge

Imagine this:

The apostle Paul himself, that great church founder and father of the first century, personally commissions *you* with a specific apostolic assignment: to commit your life and your ministry to a frail and fledgling family of faith, an underdeveloped local church, which still remains consumed and largely conformed to the corrupt culture of the community around her.

This calling requires you to leave the comfort of a familiar environment, and relocate your family to a foreign geography and culture, for a yet-to-be-determined period of time.

Your mandate is clear: To establish a strong and effective local church (or group of churches), fit and focused on advancing the Kingdom of Heaven on the earth. A community who partners in God's purposes and lives according to their new and true identity in Christ.

Your commission is to create a climate conducive to cultivating a counter cultural community; clearly characterized by Christ-like character, correct Christian conduct, and the courageous culture of the Kingdom. A Church that is no longer consumed or conformed to the corrupt culture of Crete, but on the contrary, is captivated by the King and His Kingdom, called and commissioned by Christ as constant carriers of His love, truth and life.

Welcome to the challenge of church-planting. Welcome to the world of Titus in Crete.

Our Experience

When I was twenty-three years of age, my wife, Jaye, and I both became

convinced that God had called us to plant and parent a brand new local church in my home-town on the south coast of South Australia.

With little experience (I had never preached in a Sunday service ever before), and with no formally recognized training, credentials or credibility, we and our then ten-month-old son, Jesse, started off on the adventure of our lives.

While we had much to draw upon from those who had 'gone before us', by far the greatest lessons we have learned in this process have come from personal experience, and through personal and private encounters with the Lord along the way.

It is my hope now to share with you one of the most valuable discoveries on local church leadership that I have made.

A truth that radically shifted the *focus and emphasis of my preaching ministry* as a church pastor and pioneer, and helped me to come to a place where my teaching would prove to be far more fruitful and 'biblically-balanced'. A revelation that came to me from a simple reading of Paul's apostolic instructions to his spiritual son, Titus.

Titus Chapter One: The Place of Biblical Leadership

> "[5] The reason I left you in Crete was that you might put in order what was left unfinished and **appoint elders**... [9] (who) hold firmly to the trustworthy message as it has been taught."
>
> - Titus 1:5,9 (NIV)

The context into which this letter is written is established almost immediately.

At some point in their travels, Paul asked Titus to remain on the is-

land of Crete for an undisclosed period of time, that he may "*put in order*" certain areas of church-life that required further apostolic attention and adjustment. [1]

This infamous island community was known for its greed, deceit and brutality. A sentiment noted by pagan poets of the day, and echoed here by Paul himself. [2]

However Paul's criticism is not essentially directed at the Cretan community or culture as a whole, but is specifically targeted at particular religious people (of Jewish persuasion) within the Cretan community. Experience had taught Paul that such men and their trouble-making, Gospel-distorting antics, were to be taken very seriously, and strongly guarded against.

His concern lay with the fact that the newly-formed church in Crete was in danger of being hoodwinked by heresy, taken off course by those among and around them who "*claim to know God*" but actually, in both behavior and belief, "*deny Him*". [3]

In this opening chapter, Paul's main directive is for his colleague to ensure that the local church in Crete is *led well.*

Such leadership is to be provided not by some outside organization or institutional system, but by locally based and apostolically commissioned elders/overseers, who effectively model the culture of God's Kingdom as demonstrated by their character, conduct, and convictions.

Of particular note, is that these leaders were to hold fast and firm to something Paul describes as "*the trustworthy message*". A unique term, repeated in Chapter Three, referring specifically to the message of God's grace. [4]

Clearly, Paul believed it imperative that both Titus, and subsequently the entire Christian community, possessed an adequate understanding of the role, responsibilities and requirements of those who were called to church leadership.

I agree entirely.

My wife and I often remark, with great gratitude, how blessed we have been to have spent our most formative years as young adults in a church environment which embraced a strong leadership-culture. Established largely by a deliberate emphasis on leadership teaching and training. Without this, we would most certainly never have found the grace or 'space' to plant a church in our twenties, and certainly not without formally recognized qualifications!

Biblical leadership is an essential and non-negotiable component to the health and subsequent effectiveness of the local church.

In my opinion, those who attempt to embrace an ecclesiology (a church expression/experience) with *no human leadership in place*, fall into the same error as the Pharisees whom Jesus rebuked in Matthew 15v1-9, by establishing a practice that makes aspects of God's Word "*void*" to them.

Scripture makes it clear that Jesus Himself has ordained and orchestrated His Church on the earth to be led by shepherds, built by architects, overseen by elders, coached, trained, equipped and parented by those supernaturally selected and divinely endowed with governmental graces and leadership leanings. [5]

And of course, not just any form of leadership will do... these are, after all, the people Jesus gave His life for! The responsibility to provide His Church with governmental service is indeed a "*noble task*", and those entrusted with it are to exemplify the essence of Christian maturity in their life; as the Scriptures, here in Titus Chapter One and elsewhere, make repeatedly clear. [6]

However, as important as the preaching and practice of biblical leadership may be, and while it is the first instruction Paul presents to his colleague, it is not the *main thing* the apostle directs Titus to give his attention to. There is *something else* of greater value. Something else worthy of *greater emphasis* in Titus' ministry. Something of much higher importance to the health of the Cretan Church, that demands more concentrated attention from those, like Titus, who lead and feed her.

Titus Chapter Two: The Place of Instructional Lifestyle Teaching

> "But as for you, **promote the kind of living** that reflects right teaching... they must show themselves to be entirely trustworthy and good. Then they will make the teaching about God our Savior attractive in every way."
>
> - Titus 2v1,10 (NLT)

As important as Paul's *initial* instruction may have been, Titus' ministry on Crete was not to be dedicated solely to the identification and ordination of church leaders.

The apostle now spends almost this entire second chapter (and the first two verses of the next) presenting a graphic portrayal of how 'Kingdom Culture' manifests itself in the lives of believers from all spheres of life.

Living "*self-controlled, upright and godly lives in this present age*" is not an expectation limited exclusively to those elders spoken of in the previous chapter. Rather, the grace-empowered life of eagerness to "*do what is good*" is one available and accessible to *all Christians*. Young and old, male and female, slave and free... all alike, as recipients of God's saving grace, are now both empowered and expected to conduct their day-to-day lives in a "*godly*" (i.e. Christ-like) manner. [7]

And so, what role was Titus to play in this regard?

Essentially, Paul's next major instruction to Titus is to make certain that he both *explains, models* and then *reminds* the people of what counter-cultural Christianity looks like. Through this passage, we see the use of the words *teach*, *train*, *encourage*, *rebuke*, and *remind*, as Paul makes clear that Titus' task in that church community is quite simply to instruct the believers in very practical ways, on *how they should live*. [8]

Now, please note the all-important reason *why*...

The *reason* Titus was to teach, encourage and remind these believers to manifest virtues such as self-control, temperance, reverence, kindness, integrity, peaceableness and humility, was in order that *others would be drawn to the Gospel*, and ultimately to the great and glorious God who authored it!

The motivation and purpose behind them living "*upright and godly lives*", was so that they did not "*malign the word of God*" in their community, but rather served to make His Gospel "*attractive*" to those around them. [9]

You see, the idea that our behavior and conduct somehow determines *God's* view, opinion and endorsement (or rejection) of us, is preposterous. This very concept is anti-Gospel, and is an ideology that Paul fought strongly to condemn. But Paul is not concerning himself here with *God's view* of the Christians in Crete – rather with the reputation they held in the eyes of the community around them!

Think of it this way; in John 17v4, Jesus said that He had brought the Father "*glory on earth by completing the work*" God had given Him. Now, what work was Jesus talking about here? After all, He hadn't yet been beaten and bruised for our sickness, nailed to the Cross for our sin, or raised to life for our justification. Nor had He yet sat down at the right hand of the Majesty in Heaven, or sent the Holy Spirit as promised... there was plenty more work for Jesus to do!

What work was it exactly, that He claimed to have "*completed*" prior to His arrest, which had brought His Father such glory? Fortunately, Jesus Himself answers this question for us when He says in verse 6: "*I have revealed you to those whom you gave me...*"

The same is true for us.

As representatives of our Father, we bring glory to God on the earth when we accurately reflect and effectively reveal Him to others. When we, the manifested sons of God, use both our lips and our lifestyle to make His Name and nature known to His creation.

Here in Titus Two, we discover that part of this preacher's task on Crete, was to help the believers come to an understanding of what it meant to represent God well in practical everyday living.

To suggest somehow that church leaders have *no place* in instructing fellow believers in godly conduct, or in presenting teaching that encourages Christians to live in virtuous ways, is a very difficult position to uphold in light of Scriptures such as this. Quite clearly, 'instructional lifestyle teaching' was a task the apostle Paul took upon himself, and as we see here with Titus, a responsibility he placed upon fellow leaders and ministry colleagues. [10]

Personally, I am forever grateful to have been exposed to men and women of faith over the years, who by both their teaching and testimony, have demonstrated to me what Christ-likeness can (and does) look like. I

have been blessed and inspired by preaching and teaching that has encouraged me to pursue a lifestyle of godliness (manifested in both morality and the miraculous), knowing that doing so represents my Father and His Gospel well on the earth and consequently, brings glory to His Name.

Like the preaching and practice of biblical leadership (from Titus Chapter One), instructional teaching on how Christians should live their lives in order to glorify God on the earth, is an important component to the health and subsequent effectiveness of the local church.

However, as relevant as this may be, again it is not the *main thing* that Paul directs Titus to give his attention to. There is something else of greater value still. Something else Titus was to preach and proclaim with far *greater emphasis* than instructional lifestyle teaching. Something vitally important to the ongoing health and effectiveness of the Cretan Church, that Paul – under the inspiration of Holy Spirit – commands Titus to *constantly and consistently communicate* to the Christian community...

Titus Chapter Three: The Place of Grace

> "...having been justified by his grace, we might become heirs having the hope of eternal life. This is a trustworthy saying. And I want you to **stress these things**... these things are excellent and profitable for everyone."
>
> - Titus 3v7-8 (NIV)

One of the most valuable lessons I have learnt in my years of founding and fathering a church, is the need to find a healthy balance in both my personal life and pastoral ministry.

Now, when I use the term "balance" I want you to think of it in the same way that health professionals would prescribe and promote a *balanced diet.* For a body to be healthy, it requires a well-balanced intake of a variety of foods and beverages. To have a well-balanced diet does *not* mean we treat all food types with equal importance, but rather that we understand our bodies require more of certain foods than others, and that we need to *emphasize and prioritize* accordingly.

In the same way, one major aspect of my role as a pastor/shepherd, is to "*feed (Jesus') lambs*". Much of which is done via preaching and teaching. [11] The point is, for a church to receive a healthy balance in their doctrinal diet, it is imperative that certain truths are emphasized more than others.

Here in Titus Chapter Three, Paul reaches the climax of his apostolic instruction to his spiritual son. As Jesus did at the wedding in Cana, he saves the best and most valuable wine until last! In a statement reminiscent of his first letter to the Corinthian believers, Paul waits until the end of this epistle to emphasize that which is *most important.* [12]

In order to turn the Christian community of Crete right-side-up; to establish her as a shining beacon of God's life, love and light in that community, fit and focused on devoting themselves to "*doing what is good*" and being increasingly productive in their Christian witness, Paul presses upon Titus to give his time, effort and energy to "*stress*" the Gospel. [13]

Ultimately and most importantly, Titus' task was to *constantly and consistently affirm* the true and trustworthy message of God's grace to those who had already received it! [14]

Writes Paul:

> "[3] At one time we too were foolish, disobedient, deceived and enslaved by all kinds of passions and pleasures. We lived in malice and envy, being hated and hating one another. [4] But when the kindness and love of God our Savior appeared, [5] he saved us, not because of righteous

things we had done, but because of his mercy. He saved us through the washing of rebirth and renewal by the Holy Spirit, [6] whom he poured out on us generously through Jesus Christ our Savior, [7] so that, having been justified by his grace, we might become heirs having the hope of eternal life. [8] This is a trustworthy saying. And I want you to **stress these things**..."

- Titus 3v3-8 (NIV)

"And it is on **these subjects** that I desire you to **lay special stress**..."

- Titus 3v8 (TCNT)

"...and concerning **these things** I want you to **insist steadfastly**..."

- Titus 3v8 (AMP)

"...and **these things** I want you to **affirm constantly...**"

- Titus 3v8 (NKJV)

This passage of Scripture is without question one of my very favorites.

Firstly, for its obvious personal relevance and encouragement, and secondly as a clear apostolic articulation of what I believe my preaching and teaching ministry is to be characterized by.

The theological truths contained within this "*trustworthy saying*", including the depths of our pre-Christ depravity, the solid solution of God's loving kindness, saving mercy, and unbreakable gift of justification as revealed in the Gospel, together with the generous outpouring of His Spirit and eternal inheritances that belong to us, both now and forevermore, breathe life and hope to the most despairing of souls.

But the revelation that these truths – in summary, *the glorious Gospel of God's grace* – was to be *the constant emphasis* of my ministry, would change the shape and strength of my preaching and teaching forever. [15]

Before this simple understanding, I have to confess that the emphasis of my ministry to our church was not the Gospel of Christ. Due largely to the spiritual diet on which I was feeding myself at the time, for years, my preaching and teaching to others was characterized by long lists on topics such as; "Requirements for Church Leadership", "Qualities of the Church that God Desires", "The Pattern of New Testament Christianity", and so on.

When it came to the topics outlined in Titus Chapters One and Two; I was well fed, well familiar, and ready to preach up a storm!

However, unbeknownst to me at the time, I was feeding my flock a very unbalanced and unhealthy diet, that was not actually producing what I was preaching!

Thank God that by His Spirit one day, through a simple reading of this brief epistle, the wonder of His Gospel broke into my heart and head-space again!

Thank God for the wisdom He gave me to bring change to my personal diet of teaching and preaching ministry, as I turned my ear towards those who were committed to keeping the main thing the main thing; to stress that which is of first importance – the life-giving Good News of God's lavish grace in His Son, and of His extreme and incomparable generosity with His intoxicating and empowering Spirit!

In the opening verse of this epistle, Paul says that it is "*the knowledge of the truth that leads to godliness*".[16] By constantly acknowledging the simple and scandalous truth of the Gospel and all of it's glorious implications, we are empowered to look and live more and more like Jesus on the earth – to live out in our bodies who we already are in the spirit!

This is why Paul was so committed to visiting churches in foreign cit-

ies, like those in Rome, as he was "*eager to preach the Gospel*" to them. [17] The Good News of Jesus and of His great salvation, is something that Christians themselves need to constantly hear!

When writing his first epistle to the Corinthian believers, Paul spends fourteen whole chapters dealing with all the issues and concerns they had raised with him, and one-by-one he graciously addressed them all. Then finally, he begins to draw his letter to a close by sharing what was heavily on his heart for them to hear, when he says:

> "[1] Now, brothers, **I want to remind you of the Gospel** I preached to you... [3] for what I received, I passed on to you as of **first importance**: that Christ died for our sins..."
>
> \- 1 Corinthians 15v1,3 (NIV)

While all their issues certainly mattered to Paul, the critical issue of his concern was that these believers stay grounded in the Gospel of Grace!

When Jesus told the story of the forgiving money-lender, and related it to the woman worshipping Him so extravagantly as she wept onto His feet, He made the point that those who understand they are forgiven much, will demonstrate great acts of love and worship in return. Similarly, Peter tells us that those who fail to constantly grow in qualities of Christian maturity, do so because they have lost sight of the wonder of their great salvation and the forgiveness therein. [18]

Is it no wonder that Paul's advice to Titus reflected this understanding?

Suddenly, I saw it. And my hope is that you do too.

It is understanding and encountering the grace of God that empowers godly living in His people. And so, my primary role as a shepherd to His flock, is to regularly lead them to that life-giving flow... to constantly and consistently communicate to His children the wondrous truths of the Gospel of God's grace.

That despite their background and behavior, Almighty God has, in His infinite kindness and loving mercy, completely saved, justified and purified them as His own perfect people. That He has graciously given us an eternal inheritance in which we may now participate, the guarantee of life eternal, and the ongoing generosity of the outpouring of His Spirit.

This truly is a message worthy of trust; a message deserving of regular repetition and ruthless reminding.

A Final Word

Dear reader, from today I would encourage you to take greater personal responsibility for your own spiritual diet and ministry intake. Feed on those truths which God Himself deems to be of greatest value for a healthy spiritual life. After all, while all Scripture is equally true, not all truths are equally important to the overall health of the Christian or his community. Certain truths demand greater emphasis than others, it's as simple as that.

And to those of us who find ourselves undertaking the great privilege of 'feeding' God's flock, of preaching and teaching God's Word, in whatever form or capacity; please walk in step with the eternally wise Spirit, under the counsel of His infallibly true Scriptures, and keep the main thing the main thing.

Stress the Gospel.

Constantly communicate the "*trustworthy message*" of His glorious grace.

Many responsibilities we may have, but surely none are more important than this.

"However, I consider my life worth nothing to me; my only aim is to finish the race and complete the task the Lord Jesus has given me – **the task of testifying to the good news of God's grace.**"

- Acts 20v24 (NIV)

Selah.

Endnotes

1. The NKJV renders this phrase: "...that you should set in order the things that are lacking". The AMP states: "... that you might set right what was defective *and* finish what was left undone..."

2. Note Titus 1v12-13. Greek historian Polybius (ca. 200-118BC) noted: "(it is) almost impossible to find... personal conduct more treacherous or public policy more unjust than in Crete". (Histories 6.47)

3. See Titus 1v10-16, 2v15, 3v9-11.

4. When this somewhat unique phrase *pistos logos* (sometimes translated *"faithful word"* or *"true saying"*) occurs again in Chapter 3v8, it is referring to the foundational and fundamental message of the Gospel.

5. See, for example, John 21v15-17; Acts 1v20-26, 6v1-7, 14v23, 20v17-35; Romans 12v6-8; 1 Corinthians 3v9-10; Ephesians 4v11-13; Philippians 1v1; 1 Thessalonians 2v6-12; 1 Timothy 5v17-18; Hebrews 13v7,17.

6. For similar texts related to this subject see Matthew 20v25-28, 23v1-12; Acts 20v17-35; 1 Timothy 3v1-15, 5v17-20; 1 Peter 5v1-4.

7. See Titus 2v11-14. It is worth noting that the *"grace of God that brings salvation"* is the same grace that *"teaches us"* in godly living... ie the same grace that saves us, subsequently serves to sanctify us.

8. See Titus 2v7-8,15; 3v1-2.

9. See Titus 2v5,10; 3v14.

10. From Paul see Romans 12v9-13v14; 2 Corinthians 8v1-8; Ephesians 4v25-5v21; Colossians 3v5-4v6; 1 Thessalonians 4v1-12. And from Paul advising others to do the same see 1 Timothy 3v14-15, 6v17-19; Titus 2v1-3v2, 3v14.

11. John 22v15-17; 1 Timothy 5v17. Note that in 1 Peter 5v1-4, the apostle appeals to the elders/overseers to "*be shepherds*" of God's flock, in light of Jesus our Chief and Good Shepherd (John 10v1-18; 1 Peter 2v25). This word is subsequently translated "*pastor*" in Ephesians 4v11.

12. John 1v1-11; 1 Corinthians 15v1-5.

13. Titus 3v8,14.

14. The term, "*to stress*", is the Greek word *diabebaimoomai,* meaning to asseverate; to assert and affirm a thing confidently and constantly. Interestingly, it

appears only twice in the New Testament. Here, where Titus is instructed to stress the Gospel; and, in direct contrast, once more in 1 Timothy 1v7, as a warning against those who confidently affirm the law.

15. Note: While the phrase "*the Gospel of God's grace*" may only appear once in Scripture, and is but one of some half-dozen varying terms used in the New Testament to describe the Good News of Jesus, it is nevertheless the one Paul felt most fitting when describing the message he was to testify to as his ultimate "*task*" in life (Acts 20v24).

16. Titus 1v1. Note that elsewhere the New Testament describes the Gospel as the "*word of truth*" (Ephesians 1v13; Colossians 1v5; James 1v18). In other words, it is knowing the Gospel that "*leads to godliness*".

17. Romans 1v15.

18. See Luke 7v36-50; 2 Peter 1v5-9.

Chapter 10

A Case for Divine Complacency

by John Crowder

Fully Satisfied in the Finished Work

The word "complacency" has quite a bad rap in the Church today. But I would encourage you to kick back, recline at the table and enjoy the feast as we consider the complete satisfaction Christ has provided to the believer.

Old puritan preachers, and many classic revivalists were strong proponents of divine contentment – when you read the words of Charles Spurgeon, Jonathan Edwards and others, the term "complacency" was used often. It was considered a virtue.

Edwards wrote,

> "Since I came to this town [Northampton], I have often had sweet complacency in God in views of his glorious perfections, and the excellency of Jesus Christ. God has appeared to me, a glorious and lovely being chiefly on account of his holiness. The holiness of God has always appeared to me the most lovely of all his attributes." [1]

R.C. Sproul points to Edwards' use of the word *complacency* in its basic Oxford Dictionary definition as, "The fact or state of being pleased with a thing or person; tranquil pleasure or satisfaction in something or some one." Adds Sproul, "I labor the earlier English usage of the word *complacency* because it is used in a crucial manner in the language of historic, orthodox theology."

Sproul writes:

> "If we take note of Edwards' language, his choice of words to describe his enraptured delight in the glory of God, we observe his accent on the sweetness, loveliness, and excellence of God. He reports of enjoying a 'sweet complacency' in God. What does he mean? Is not the term complacency a word we use to describe a certain

> smugness, a resting on one's laurels, a sort of lazy inertia that attends a superficial sort of satisfaction? Perhaps. But here we see a vivid example of how words sometimes change their import over time." [2]

What Edwards meant by a "*sweet complacency*" had nothing to do with a contemporary dose of smugness. Rather, it had to do with a sense of pleasure. This "pleasure" is not to be understood in a crass hedonistic, or sensual, sense but rather a delight in that which is supremely pleasing to the soul.

The Key to Contentment

Holy complacency is all about being satisfied in the divine pleasures of God.

> "They will be intoxicated with the fatness of your house, and you will give them drink from the wadi of your delights, because with you is life's fountain; in your light we shall see light."
>
> - Psalm 36:8 (Septuagint)

In writing to the Philippian Church, Paul urges them to be anxious about nothing (Philippians 4:6) and presents himself as an example of a man who has learned to be content in times of plenty and in seasons of external lack (Philippians 4:11-13). How did Paul muster up this contentment?

Traditional religionists will strive for the *annihilation of desire.* But that is gnostic stoicism – okay for a Buddhist, but not for a Christian. Paul did not learn to desire less, so he could be content with less. In fact, the apostle's appetites were hot and furious, not lessened. Although fulfillment to those desires came neither through worldly ambition, nor his own religious efforts.

Paul had learned to be fully satisfied on the fatty ashes of Christ's sacrifice.

> "I will satisfy fully the life of the priests with abundance, and My people will be satisfied with My goodness, says the Lord."
>
> - Jeremiah 31:14 (NIV)

> "Blessed (happy, fortunate, to be envied) is the man whom You choose and cause to come near, that he may dwell in Your courts! We shall be satisfied with the goodness of Your house, Your holy temple."
>
> - Psalm 65:4 (AMP)

Paul found everything he had ever wanted in the person of Christ – the source of his bliss and fulfillment. Those in Christ truly *lack nothing.* He had been plugged into an eternal wellspring of grace.

Maybe this satisfaction – this divine complacency – sounds good to you on paper. But how do we tangibly feast on this abundant grace in our daily lives? By faith. That is, simply by *trusting.* The flavor of faith is not striving, contending or "pressing in" for something. The flavor of faith is *rest.* It is to trust in what someone else has already accomplished for us. His work was enough to satisfy you perfectly.

Christ has now become our eternal *Sabbath rest.*

Satisfied with the Sin Remedy

Staunch legalists, strivers, and will-power advocates get itchy when you speak too often of grace. They are hell-bent on ridding the Church of the wrong type of complacency. Their fear is that you will promote the ever-taboo notion of *greasy grace.* But I'll be the first to say that grace is far greasier than anyone would have suspected! Slippery, buttery and dripping with ease and fatness – no one could exaggerate how free and glorious this

grace is. Grace is not cheap – it cost Jesus everything.

Your own everything couldn't afford it.

However, if we are speaking in terms of "license to sin," that is where the misconception about grace lies. Grace is not simply a "hiding" away of sin – or even a mere *forgiveness* of your sinfulness. Grace is not just a cover up – as if God, the great Santa Claus in the sky, is covering his eyes from your wrongdoings – acting as if they don't exist. He's not choosing to put you on the "nice" list when you deserve the "naughty" list. Grace does not hide God's eyes from your sinfulness. That's what we've been taught – but the true Gospel is far better.

Grace actually *eradicates* sinfulness itself. It's not a cover up – instead, it's an absolute removal of your old heart. Grace is not a freedom *to sin*, but it is freedom *from sin*. On the Cross, your sinfulness itself was destroyed in His death. Your old sinful self was co-crucified together with Christ. Grace mystically transformed your identity from a sinner to a saint. There's no mixture left.

Grace does not merely "cut you slack" while leaving you with *indwelling sinfulness*. Grace fully nailed that indwelling sinfulness to the tree – your entire old corrupt nature was abolished as a free gift (Romans 6; Galatians 2:20).

What I am saying is that there is nothing left for you to do, but simply *be who you are* – that perfect new you who is *one spirit with the Lord* (1 Corinthians 6:17). Now your chief end is to glorify God, simply by enjoying Him forever. As John Piper often says, "God is most glorified in you when you are most satisfied in Him."

Does Grace Produce Apathy?

Keeping these things in mind, we must depart from the ridiculous, but sadly common misconception that *grace breeds sinfulness.* This was the same faulty argument that Paul addressed concerning his Judaizing opponents in Galatians 2. For the Jews to admit their need of grace, was an admission of the inadequacy of the law to justify them. The law, being found insufficient, was therefore abandoned as a justifying agency. To invalidate the law – did this mean that Christ therefore was a promoter of sin?

> "If, while we seek to be justified in Christ, it becomes evident that we ourselves are sinners, does that mean that Christ promotes sin? Absolutely not!"
>
> - Galatians 2:17 (NIV)

Let me explain this tricky verse from the top. Paul is not suggesting that "*we*" believers must continually *seek justification* – nor is he saying here that believers are *still sinners.* He is speaking of those who are still bound in religion, who have not yet found the complacent satisfaction of their perfection in Christ. Bible translator Kenneth Wuest opens up this verse:

> "The Christian Jews, in seeking to be justified in Christ, were shown to be sinners just like and in the same class as the Gentiles. When they sought justification in Christ and thus by grace, it was an admission on their part that there is no justification by works, that the seeker is not justified, and is therefore a sinner. The attempt to be justified in Christ awakens the consciousness of sin, and compels the Jew to put himself on the plane of the Gentile. The Jew who calls the Gentile a sinner, in seeking to be justified by faith, is forced to admit that he is a sinner also. He has found that the law has failed him as a justifying agency.

> Paul repudiates the false assumption of the Judaizers who charged that Christ is the promoter and encourager of sin in that He causes the Jew to abandon the law as a justifying agency, and in doing so, puts himself on the common plane of a Gentile whom he calls a sinner and a dog. The Judaizers argued that in view of the fact that violation of the law is sin, therefore, abandonment of the law in an effort to be justified in Christ is also sin. Thus Christ is the promoter of sin." [3]

It is the law that *increases sin.* Does grace cause sin? Absolutely not! Paul writes, "*The law was added so that the trespass might increase. But where sin increased, grace increased all the more,*" (Romans 5:20). Paul also asks in Romans 6:1, "*What shall we say then? Shall we keep on sinning since grace abounds? Perish the thought! How shall we who died to sin keep doing that very thing?*" The renowned Bible commentator, Martyn Lloyd Jones, wrote:

> "The true preaching of the gospel of salvation by grace alone always leads to the possibility of this charge being brought against it. There is no better test as to whether a man is really preaching the New Testament gospel of salvation than this, that some people might misunderstand it and misinterpret it to mean that it really amounts to this, that because you are saved by grace alone it does not matter at all what you do; you can go on sinning as much as you like because it will redound all the more to the glory of grace. If my preaching and presentation of the gospel of salvation does not expose it to that misunderstanding, then it is not the gospel." [4]

I don't want to overcomplicate this. But I had to lay some groundwork for a very simple idea. Grace does not amplify the drive to sin – religion does that. More specifically, grace does not incite the one specific sin it is most often blamed for – the sin of *apathy.*

Grace does not cause apathy – religion does.

Retiring from Self-Effort

Let me put this in simple terms now. Someone will say, "If you preach grace, people are going to get lazy."

True grace does not produce laziness, but it does breed divine complacency!

The common mindset is that everyone will clock out if we aren't motivating them with fear, guilt and religion. This is the sick perversion that has masqueraded as Christianity far too long. It is bondage – the spirit of antichrist at work in the pulpit, and is diametrically opposed to the Gospel.

True grace does not promote apathy or "self-complacency". It is not freedom to be apathetic – grace is freedom *from apathy*. Paul had a fiery ambition that drove him preaching all over the Mediterranean, from Jerusalem to northern Greece, until there was *no place left for him to preach* (Romans 15:23). He was an Energizer Bunny! But Paul was not motivated by anything less than the enjoyment of God and the fire of love that burned in his bones. He said, "*Woe to me if I don't preach the gospel,*" (1 Corinthians. 9:16). He felt a glorious compulsion – an inward fulfillment and delight from spreading this good news. He couldn't stop himself – he was possessed by the love of God which "compelled" him. The grace apostle achieved far more than the rest.

Paul's compulsion to serve did not originate from a slavish need to "help God out". He co-labored only in a sense that he was a 'container' of God. The branch passively drinks the sap of the vine and effortlessly bears fruit as a result of its union. This is more than simple semantics. Instead of Christ *with Paul* – it was Christ *as Paul.*

> "For it is God which worketh in you both to will and to do of his good pleasure."
>
> - PHILIPPIANS. 2:13 (KJV)

God does not need your efforts to help prop Him up. Though you serve and do things for the kingdom in this life, yet it is no longer you, but Christ laboring *through* you, "*according to the working of his mighty power*" (Ephesians 1:19). You are living in a state of active retirement. The *you* is retired, and now the Christ has replaced you. You are simply a vessel, a temple – a container that holds this mighty God.

> "I consider myself as having died and now I'm enjoying a new existence which is simply Jesus using my body."
>
> - GALATIANS 2:20 (DISTILLED BIBLE)

Even Christ's continued work through your life is to *announce the Gospel* – that is, the good news that His work has been finished since the foundation of the world. Your entire life proclaims an already completed victory!

Jesus actually meant it when He said, "*It is finished.*" He didn't just mean it's finished for *that day.* "Wow. It's been really tough at the office boys – I'm gonna knock off early and call it a day. Be back again at 9 AM to start this all over again!"

The finished work of the Cross is such an offense, because it invalidates every other human attempt at spirituality. Though we labor to proclaim the Cross, we do not labor to repeat it as religion does. We do not labor to strive toward our own holiness, sanctification, or redemption. We just believe it's ours. Nor do we strive to enter into more of His fullness. For *by our union with Christ we are already full of the Godhead* (Colossians 2:10).

A Better Kind of Complacency

There's a massive difference between the pleasant satisfaction of divine complacency and the numbing paralysis of lukewarm nominalism. We've all seen churches that are dead cold – no excitement, no zealous fervor for the Lord. Their joy and expectancy are sucked dry. They slumber.

The problem of apathy is real, and many John the Baptist types try to address it. It is no wonder that so many, who have caught the fire of the Spirit, want to shake and rock the Church back to attention. To rouse her from her narcotized sleep.

And so, what do these zealous trumpets do? Unfortunately, they try to get Mother Church off the couch and right onto the treadmill. They bark at her. They shout at her. They come at her with the whip of the law. To their credit, these voices *do have zeal*, but it is a zeal "*without knowledge*" of grace as Paul says in Romans 10 – zeal for self-effort. Pharisees are very zealous. The answer to apathy is not zeal for the law. Instead, we need a zealous appreciation that Christ has finished the job. John the Baptist was great, but there has been a change in covenant.

Grace does not beat the Church awake. Grace woos her with the extravagant love of Christ poured out on the Cross, entices her with the fragrant myrrh of His sufferings for her on the Cross. It allures her with the promise of divine pleasures that supersede the lesser comforts of this world, and invites her to drink and to be drunk on love (Song of Solomon 5:1).

Hunger versus Satisfaction

In the face of overwhelming apathetic disinterest in the Church, many charismatic zealots feel justified in whipping people up into a striving frenzy, *"We've got to get hungry! We've got to get desperate! We have to cry out for more! We must press in for revival!"*

There is an inward striving, an internal hernia-popping to push themselves into something they already have. Religion always gets you to work for something that's already yours.

In fear of growing lukewarm – they say we must constantly stay *hungry for God.* Intimacy with God becomes a striving work. Such a person tries to remain in a state of *dissatisfaction* at their current "level" of spirituality. As if by forcing themselves to be unhappy, they will be pleasing to God. Meanwhile, that old virtue of divine contentment in Christ's fullness gets thrown out the window. This whole thing is actually rooted in a *lack* of faith.

I'm not *pressing in* anymore. I've been pressed into.

I'm not *contending* anymore. I've been contended for.

I'm not a *God chaser* anymore. I've been chased down, roped, and hog-tied. Bagged and tagged!

So many fast; they pray; they push; they pull. They attempt to get what they've already got. But their own efforts have alienated them from grace.

I'm not *hungry* anymore. I am fully satisfied.

Hunger is the state of the prodigal in the pig slop. Sonship is satisfied on Christ – the Father's fatted calf.

You may ask, "But doesn't God want us to hunger for more and more of Him? Doesn't He want us to hunger and thirst after righteousness?"

First of all, you are already righteous in Him. But notice the rest of that verse.... He says that those who hunger will be *"fully satisfied"*.

"Blessed and fortunate and happy and spiritually prosperous (in that state in which the born-again child of God enjoys His favor and salvation) are those who hunger and thirst for righteousness (uprightness and right standing with God), for they shall be completely satisfied!"

- MATTHEW 5:6 (AMP)

Our satisfaction speaks of trusting and drinking from all that He has done. The flavor of faith is not thirst, the flavor of faith is *complete satisfaction*, knowing that we sit at the King's table. This is what Abraham, the father of faith, was commended for. He was,

"Fully satisfied and assured that God was able and mighty to keep His word and to do what He had promised."

- ROMANS 4:21 (AMP)

Religious people know that money, material things, and the work of their hands don't bring contentment. But they do think that their striving to please God and follow the rules will bring satisfaction. They're looking to add something onto the Cross for extra brownie points. They don't see that they are still basing their hope of satisfaction on *self.*

Are you fully satisfied in what He has done? Or are you still praying, "More Lord"?

A Language of Unbelief

There is a prevailing language of unbelief in the Charismatic Church today. A barrage of terminology and ideas that lock people into a never-ending search for God. The point of conversion was not your initiation rite into a lifelong chase after an elusive, fleeting deity. We are not called to be God-chasers, always begging for a little bit more like Oliver Twist. I am no longer even "seeking after God". He has found me. He and I are in *unio mystica.*

The New Covenant is a finding covenant. An arrival. An enjoyment of the Promised Land that we have already entered. Isn't your claim to Christianity the very boast that you are no longer looking for answers, but that you have found Him? Christianity is the only religion that can scandalously boast that we are no longer seeking, but have confidently laid hold of God. It seems such an arrogant boast! "I have *all* of God! I have arrived!" This is the stumbling block of the ages.

Seeking is a pre-Christ action.

One would say, "But doesn't He reward those who earnestly seek Him?" That is Hebrews 11:6. Read the beginning of the verse, "*And without faith it is impossible to please God.*" God is impressed with faith. Believe that you are in union with Him by the finished work of the Cross.

The Lord once spoke to an anonymous mystic, asking her this, "If I am the air you breathe, if you are in Me and I am in you, why are you looking for Me?" She said, "At once I felt so close to God that I could never describe it. …"[5]

Never again fall for those catch phrases of today, prompting you to "get hungry" for God. How can I do that, when I've been feasting on the Lamb? The admission of hunger is an admission of lack. A hungry child is a sign of bad parenting. It is an assertion that Christ's sacrifice was not a good enough meal for you. Do you need something more than His Cross? Let the Cross be the only thing that mesmerizes you. Stop begging for things He's already given. Stop asking from an Old Covenant perspective. He has already poured out all that Heaven has to offer.

There's no more need to beg Him to "*open the Heavens*". He already did

that. He checked that one right off the prayer list when the veil of His flesh was torn and all of Heaven opened with it. If you stop asking for that – and actually believe it exists for you – you will experience that open Heaven every day of your life. A fully supernatural lifestyle.

Are you tired of a performance-based, emotional roller coaster type of spirituality, thinking God is happy with you one day and upset with you the next? Trust in His finished work, not your own efforts. Rest in the knowledge that you are permanently plugged into Heaven, whether you know it or not, feel it or not. He is continually smiling at you. You are basking in permaglory thanks to His work. Don't doubt just because you're not experiencing it. It is by first believing that we experience. Manifestations *follow* faith.

> "As for me, I will continue beholding Your face in righteousness (rightness, justice, and right standing with You); I shall be fully satisfied, when I awake [to find myself] beholding Your form [and having sweet communion with You]."
>
> - Psalm 17:15 (AMP)

There is an infinitely sweet satisfaction in beholding His face. And how does the believer do this? Because the veil of sinfulness has been removed, we can see Him clearly in the person of Christ. He told of this day long ago through the prophet, "*I will no longer hide my face from them, for I will pour out my Spirit...* " (Ezekiel 39:29)

> "My whole being shall be satisfied as with marrow and fatness; and my mouth shall praise You with joyful lips."
>
> - Psalm 63:5 (NKJV)

And so we come to the real root of the issue. Renowned 17th century theologian, Jeremy Taylor, once quipped, "*God threatens terrible things if we will not be happy.*" God demands joy. God demands that we be satisfied. God demands that we be fat and complacent on the very thing that He is fat and complacent upon. Again, Sproul says:

> "God's love of complacency is the special delight and pleasure He takes first of all in His only-begotten Son. It is Christ who is the beloved of the Father, supremely; He is the Son in whom the Father is 'well pleased.'"

By adoption in Christ, every believer shares in this divine love of complacency. It is the love enjoyed by Jacob, but not by Esau. This love is reserved for the redeemed in whom God delights – not because there is anything inherently lovely or delightful in us – but we are so united to Christ, the Father's Beloved, that the love the Father has for the Son spills over onto us. God's love for us is pleasing and sweet to Himself – and to us...

Endnotes

1. George Marsden, *Jonathan Edwards: A Life* (Yale University, 2003), p12.
2. R.C. Sproul, Abundant Love (Article from Tabletalk Magazine).
3. Kenneth Wuest, *Wuest Word Studies in the Greek New Testament* (William B. Eerdmans Publishing Co., 1980).
4. Dr. Martin Lloyd-Jones, *Commentary on Romans 6.*
5. Fr. Juan Arintero, *The Song of Songs: A Mystical Exposition* (Rockford, IL: Tan Books and Publishers, Inc., 1974, 1992), 403.

CHAPTER 11

The New Covenant in a Nutshell

A Fresh Look at New Covenant Truths

by Paul Hernandez

The New Covenant is the greatest and most beautiful revelation of the Scripture in a believer. It's very liberating when a believer has received – through the lenses of the New Covenant – understanding of God, the Scriptures, who we are, and the finished work of Jesus. It is a treasure that cannot be compared even to the most precious jewels.

In John 4, there is a story where Jesus sent His disciples to go and look for food, while He went to a nearby well to wait for them. A Samaritan woman came to draw water. Jesus said to her, "Will you give me a drink?" Jews did not associate with Samaritans, especially not one as bad as this lady, who had five husbands and whom the man she was with during that time was her sixth. That day, she finally met the seventh man! This woman was self and sin-conscious. She was full of herself before she met Jesus. He explained clearly to her who He really is, and in verses 13-14, he told her, "*Whoever drinks of this water will thirst again, but whoever drinks of the water that I shall give him will never thirst. The water that I shall give him will become in him a fountain of water springing up into everlasting life.*" Later in verse 21, Jesus said, "*Believe me.*" The only thing we can do to enter God's rest is to believe.

> "We who have believed enter that rest."
>
> \- Hebrews 4:3 (NIV)

> "anyone who enters God's rest also rests from their own works."
>
> \- Hebrews 4:10 (NIV)

> "Let us, therefore, make every effort to enter that rest."
>
> \- Hebrews 4:11 (NIV)

The New Covenant is a covenant of believing, and that's exactly what Jesus said to the woman, "Believe me, woman."

The woman replied, "*I know that messiah (called Christ) is coming. When He comes, He will explain everything to us.*" Then Jesus said, "*I who speak to you am*

He." Of which the literal translation should be "I who speak to you *I am.*"

He is the "*I am*". Jesus said in John 8:58, *"Most assuredly, I say to you, before Abraham was, I am."* In this story, Jesus is introducing the truths of the New Covenant. He is introducing who the Father really is: A God who connects, who cleanses, who does not condemn. A God who speaks, who empowers and a God who can be worshipped without the limitations of space, tradition, or religion (John 4:21-24). I love it that in the New Covenant, we must worship in spirit and in truth. Worship is not based on the flesh, what we experience and feel with our five senses. We worship God in the spiritual realm, according to what He has accomplished in the realm of the spirit. He said in John 19:30, *"It is finished,"* and in Ephesians 1:3, *"Blessed be the God and Father of our Lord Jesus Christ, who has blessed us with every spiritual blessing in the heavenly places in Christ."* Everything that we see in the physical realm is a product of the spiritual realm.

In the spiritual realm, everything is done, has been accomplished, and is finished. We worship God in spirit and in truth.

Let me explain it in a very simple and scriptural way. In John 14:6, Jesus says, *"I am the way, the truth and the life,"* and in John 1:17, we read, *"For the law was given through Moses, but grace and truth came through Jesus Christ."* The truth is Jesus Christ!

In John 16:13, Jesus says, *"when He, the spirit of truth, comes, He will guide you into all truth."* We know that the main ministry of the Holy Spirit is to point everyone to Jesus Christ. Let me paraphrase this, "When He comes, He will guide you into all of who Jesus really is." Therefore we can conclude that John 4:24 can be translated in the New Covenant as, "We worship God in the finished work and through Jesus Christ."

Back to the story in John 4. The disciples returned and were surprised to find Jesus talking to a Samaritan woman. They had left knowing that

Jesus was hungry and tired, perhaps even sleepy, but found Him rejuvenated and refreshed upon their return. They knew that He had not eaten yet, so they urged Him, *"Rabbi, eat something,"* and He said to them, *"I have food to eat that you know nothing about."* The disciples wondered and pondered his answer. They were wondering where Jesus had found food or whether He had even eaten while they were away. Had He kept some bread hidden away?

They saw Him relaxed, rejuvenated, and refreshed. He explained in verse 34, *"My food is to do the will of Him who sent me and to finish His work."* Wow! Doing the will of God is the food that rejuvenates, refreshes, and comforts us; it is something that is stress-free, satisfying, empowering, invigorating and joyous.

> "Then He said, 'Behold, I have come to do Your will, O God.' He takes away the first that He may establish the second."
>
> - Hebrews 10:9 (NKJV)

Wow! God's will for us is to take away the first, which is the Old Covenant of the Law, and to establish the second, which is the New Covenant of Grace. Whenever we are taking away the Old Covenant and establishing the New Covenant, we are doing the will of God. It brings us to a relaxed, refreshed and continually rejuvenated mode of life and ministry. The blaze of God's glory, the bliss of His grace, and the blast of His goodness will always have this effect.

1. The New Covenant Man: Identity

The New Covenant man is full of Jesus in his life. He is submitted to, sanctified, and soaked in the presence of God and His Spirit. A New Covenant man is a man of glory, goodness, greatness and grace. He is a fountain of joy, clothed in righteousness, wrapped in peace, surrounded with favor and strengthened in the strength and power of God. As Psalm 21:6 puts it, *"You made him forever most blessed."* He is forever and supremely blessed. A New Covenant man is crowned with His glory, captured with His goodness and consumed by God's grace.

Here are some characteristics of a New Covenant Man:

1. Happiness

The New Covenant man is a happy man. The first preaching or teaching that Jesus made was about happiness.

> "Blessed are the poor in spirit, for theirs is the Kingdom of Heaven."
>
> - Matthew 5:3 (NIV)

The word "*blessed*" here comes from Greek word *makarios* which means, "Blessed, happy and to be envied."

> "Blessed is he whose transgression is forgiven, whose sin is covered. Blessed is the man to whom the LORD does not impute iniquity, and in whose spirit there is no deceit."
>
> - Psalm 32:1-2 (NKJV)

The word for "*blessed*" used here, comes from the Hebrew word *esher* which means, "happiness and blessedness". The Gospel is good news, something that makes us happy and feel good. It takes away reproach, condemnation, agitation, and accusation from within our hearts and minds.

According to the Westminster Larger Catechism of 1647, *"The chief and highest end of man is to glorify God, and to fully enjoy Him forever."*

In John 14:6, Jesus declares, "*I am the way, the truth and the life.*" Jesus is our life. John 3:16 says, "*For God so loved the world, that He gave His only begotten Son, that whoever believes in Him should not perish but have everlasting life.*" We can see that the three most sought after and fought for truths – that only grace and the person of Jesus Christ can give – are love, liberty, and life.

Love is the most sought after gift that a person can ever long for. It gives us happiness and makes us feel important and accepted.

Liberty is the most fought for state. Every one of us longs for liberty. Many have fought and died for the sake of liberty, but God has freed us from the bondage to sin and given us liberty through the finished work of the Cross.

The other thing is life, a good and blessed state that all of us dream of. A life that is filled with blessings, good health and good things.

Love, liberty and life.

Grace allows us to have them all. It makes us happy people and blessed children of our Abba Father.

2. Forgiven

Martin Luther said, *"Forgiveness of sins is the very heart of Christianity, and yet it is a mighty dangerous thing to preach."*

Forgiveness is the key towards a happy, peaceful and joyous life. When one experiences the truth of forgiveness, it opens the door to a new state of being, a life of blessings and right standing before God.

The Old Testament word "forgive" comes from two Hebrew words:

Nasa – the taking away, forgiveness or pardon of sin, inquiry and transgression.

Salah – God's offer of pardon and forgiveness to sinners.

In the New Testament, four Greek words; *aphiemi, aphesis, charizomai* and *apoluo,* are translated as "forgive":

Aphiemi – to send forth, send away, to remit or forgive debts and sins; cancel remission of guilt of sin.

Aphesis – to pardon, cancellation of a punishment or guilt, forgiveness of sins.

Charizomai – to give, equaling remit, forgive, pardon.... To release a person from the obligation of repaying what is owed.

Apoluo - Legal releasing.

> "In righteousness you shall be established; You shall be far from oppression, for you shall not fear; and from terror, for it shall not come near you."
>
> - Isaiah 54:14 (NKJV)

Being forgiven is the key to a life of manifest blessing.

> "No weapon formed against you shall prosper, and every tongue which rises against you in judgment You shall condemn. This is the heritage of the servants of the LORD, And their righteousness is from Me,' says the Lord."
>
> - Isaiah 54:17 (NKJV)

The enemy will always try to form a weapon against us, but he shall not prosper. In this verse, the weapon is in a singular form. It's the weapon of deception, condemnation, and accusation, when we listen to his lies, we put ourselves under condemnation.

> "And they overcame him by the blood of the Lamb and by the word of their testimony, and they did not love their lives to the death."
>
> - Revelation 12:11 (NKJV)

We overcome the devil's deceptions through the blood of the Lamb. Before, I thought that we could only use the blood of Jesus when we pray and rebuke the enemy, which I personally think is not a bad thing to do, but the primary purpose of the Blood is seen in the passages of Matthew 26:28 and Hebrews 9:22,

> "For this is My blood of the new covenant, which is shed for many for the remission of sins."
>
> - Matthew 26:28 (NKJV)

> "And according to the law almost all things are purified with blood, and without shedding of blood there is no remission."
>
> - Hebrews 9:22 (NKJV)

The blood of the Lamb is for the forgiveness of all our sins. We therefore say that knowing the power of the Blood, stops and takes away the power of satan's deception and condemnation in our lives. Whenever he accuses us of our sin, we remind him of the Blood that was shed for the forgiveness and remission of all our sin.

3. United with Christ

> "For if we have been united together in the likeness of His death, certainly we also shall be in the likeness of His resurrection."
>
> - Romans 6:5 (NKJV)

The word "*united*" here comes from the Greek word *sumphutos* which means, "congenital, growing together, united with." It comes from the root word *sumphuó* which means, "to grow at the same time." And the word *sumphuo* comes from the two Greek root words, *sun* which means, "with or together with," and *phuo,* which means, "to bring forth or produce". Put together they mean, "to bring forth and produce together at the same time." Now we get the words "Siamese twins", which Merriam-Webster defines as "a pair of congenitally united twins". Identical twins can live their lives without the other, but when we talk of Siamese twins, living their lives without the other is impossible. That is the wonder and mystery of our union with Christ; it is a mystical and truthful union. Jesus and I are not only together, but we are Siamese twins.

Some people think, "I'm pretty much like the good thief hanging next to Jesus on the Cross. I did some bad things, but He still saved me." No! You were not the thief that was hung next to Jesus. Your death was much more up-close and personal than that. You were mystically in Christ, hanging on His tree when He died. The same nail that pierced through His hands went through yours.

4. Righteous

> "For He made Him who knew no sin to be sin for us, that we might become the righteousness of God in Him."
>
> - 2 Corinthians 5:21 (NKJV)

We are righteous in Him, in all ways and in all aspects of our lives. Righteousness is a huge and exciting truth, but let me just dwell on one particular issue that concerns our body. I have encountered a lot of questions concerning the body (Greek: *sarx*) which some say is a dirty or unholy vessel, they understand it as a case of righteous beings dwelling in a dirty vessel. However, our bodies are created by God and are His masterpiece. When He created man, He said it was very good (Genesis 1:31). The idea that our body is sinful, that we are trapped in a dirty vessel, and the only way for us to be totally delivered is through our death, makes death more powerful than the blood. Those who say that our bodies and our flesh are of sinful nature, imply that Jesus was also living in a dirty vessel until He was crucified on the Cross.

> "Or do you not know that your body is the temple of the Holy Spirit who is in you, whom you have from God, and you are not your own?"
>
> - 1 CORINTHIANS 6:19 (NKJV)

The Holy Spirit cannot dwell in an unholy vessel. Therefore, if we are a temple of the Holy Spirit, then it is impossible that our body is a sinful or dirty vessel.

Sin was defeated when the law was nailed to the Cross (Colossians 2:14). Our sinful nature was defused when righteousness reigned and took up habitation in us (2 Corinthians 5:17). We are therefore righteous in all ways and all aspect of our lives, we are not righteous beings living in unholy or dirty vessels, but we are simply the righteousness of God in Christ Jesus.

ii. The New Covenant Thinking: Mindset

The word "*mind-set*" refers to our "mental inclination". Mental inclination is where your mind sub-consciously or unconsciously dwells, and what it believes in.

Matthew 3:2 says, "*Repent, for the kingdom of Heaven is at hand.*" That verse has been taught and preached in a wrong context, which has brought accusation, reproach, condemnation and guilt to the listener. It was understood as if God's kingdom is all about judgment and condemnation that must therefore compel us to repent of our sins. The word "repent" in the New Testament, comes from the Greek word *metanoeo* which means, "to change one's mind or purpose". It does not, therefore, talk about remorse, and is not even about sin at all. It is a mind issue. Romans 14:17 says, *"For the kingdom of God is not eating and drinking, but righteousness and peace and joy in the Holy Spirit."* We can, therefore, quote Matthew 3:2 in the following phrase, "Change your mind, for righteousness, peace and joy in the Holy Ghost is at hand."

It is a gospel of the good news of righteousness that produces peace, which in turn, produces joy. We know from Nehemiah 8:10 that, "*...the joy of the LORD is your strength,*" and in Philippians 4:13 it says, *"I can do all things through Christ who strengthens me."* We do all things through Christ's strength, which is the result of the joy of the Lord. This comes from peace which is ours through understanding our righteousness in Christ Jesus.

> "The Spirit of the Lord GOD is upon me, because the LORD has anointed me to preach good tidings to the poor; He has sent me to heal the brokenhearted, to proclaim liberty to the captives, and the opening of the prison to those who are bound; to proclaim the acceptable year of the LORD, and the day of vengeance of our God; to comfort all who mourn,"
>
> - Isaiah 61:1-2 (NKJV)

Jesus quoted this scripture in Luke 4:18-20. He read about a year of God's favor and a day of God's vengeance. Here, favor lasts for a year, while vengeance is only for a day. But notice that when Jesus read this scripture, He did not even mention "*the day of vengeance of our God,*" but instead he closed the book after reading, "*to proclaim the acceptable year of the Lord.*" This clearly shows that vengeance was never part of Jesus' ministry.

> "For God did not send His Son into the world to condemn the world, but that the world through Him might be saved."
>
> - John 3:17 (NKJV)

The New Covenant is not a covenant of judgment, but of joy; not of law, but of love; not of good works, but of grace; and not of flesh, but of faith.

Religion blinds our minds. It tries to give the impression that Heaven is far away, a place where God dwells, without us realizing that Heaven is in Jesus Christ. Religion makes everything a process and a practice, without the person of Jesus Christ. Heaven is a realm, a realm of God where His presence is present and His grace is overflowing.

Even our mentality towards sin needs to be transformed. Sin does not cause separation, but separation causes sin. Adam and Eve were deceived by the serpent, when it convinced them that they needed to do something to be like God. Through this, a spirit of independence came to their hearts and minds, the spirit of separation entered and eventually produced disobedience and sin in their actions. The same thing happened with Lucifer when he said, *"I will be like God,"* (Isaiah 14:13-14). He had a spirit of separation and independence and it produced rebellion in him. Sin is a by-product of separation and independence, not the other way around. That is why grace brings intimacy between us and the Father. It brings relationship like no other; a closeness that is authored by God Himself through His Son, Jesus Christ.

Sin is at its root not the behavior or the action itself, but a state of being. When our identity is firmly established, then we will be sure of our state and standing. We are neither striving nor struggling, but we are standing on solid ground where other grounds are sinking sands.

The Tree of the Knowledge of Good and Evil itself was not evil or sinful. God created it and it was good. Therefore, we must realize that it's not about the bad or the good, but it's the separation that makes us fall into sin. Even good things become idols upon which we put our trust and reliance. When good things become our basis for producing godliness and right standing with God, they too can become idols.

When Martin Luther realized that righteousness is a free gift of grace, it created a new life experience for him and that marked the start of the Reformation.

Mentality is very important. Particularly in our core beliefs. Our mind-set defines all of who we are, including our emotions and eventually our actions.

Here are some definitions taken from Merriam-Webster Online Dictionary that I find quite illuminating:

Mindset: A mental attitude or inclination, a fixed state of mind.

Mentality: A mental power or capacity, a mode or way of thought.

Imagination: The act or power of forming a mental image of something not present to the senses, or never before wholly perceived in reality.

Rationalization: To bring into accord with reason, or cause something to seem reasonable.

Thinking: The action of one's mind to achieve or produce thought.

Logic: Formally true or valid.

Understanding: The power of comprehending.

Comprehension: The capacity for understanding fully.

Grasp: To make the motion of seizing.

Knowledge: The fact or condition of being aware of something.

Wisdom: The ability to discern.

Mind-set can either build or break us.

> "My people are destroyed **for lack of knowledge**. Because you have rejected knowledge, I also will reject you from being priest for Me;

Because you have forgotten the law of your God, I also will forget your children."

- Hosea 4:6 (NKJV)

Mind-set can either bless or beat us.

"And truly if they had **called to mind** that country from which they had come out, they would have had opportunity to return. But now they desire a better, that is, a heavenly country. Therefore God is not ashamed to be called their God, for He has prepared a city for them."

-Hebrews 11:15-16 (AMP)

Mind-set can either brighten or blind us.

"I beseech you therefore, brethren, by the mercies of God, that you present your bodies a living sacrifice, holy, acceptable to God, which is your reasonable service. [2] And do not be conformed to this world, but be transformed by the renewing of your mind, that you may prove what is that good and acceptable and perfect will of God."

- Romans 12:1-2 (NKJV)

Helen Keller once said, "The worst person that ever lived is a person who has sight, yet is without vision."

"This I say, therefore, and testify in the Lord, that you should no longer walk as the rest of the Gentiles walk, in the futility of their mind,"

- Ephesians 4:17 (NKJV)

Ephesians 4:23 says, "*to be made new in the attitude of the mind*". Gentiles walk in the futility of their minds, but the believers walk with a renewed mind, a mind that is Jesus conscious.

Let me make some comparisons between an Old Covenant and New Covenant mentality:

OLD COVENANT	NEW COVENANT
I seek God.	God sought me. Luke 19:10
I pray to God for revival.	I am the revival. John 6:58
I believe for blessings.	I am the blessed and I am the blessing of God. Ephesians 1:3
I need to earn God's blessings.	God's blessings have earned and saved me. Romans 2:4
I look for an open Heaven.	I am God's open heaven (I can release miracles & healing). Mark 16:17-18
I am looking for the move of God.	I am the very move of God (God is in you). Philippians 4:13; Colossians 1:27
I need to obey to be blessed.	I am already blessed and it empowers me to obey. Titus 2:10-11; Titus 3:8; Romans 1:5
I need to be forgiven.	I am already forgiven. Colossians 3:13; Ephesians 4:32
I chase the anointing.	I have the anointing of Jesus Christ. 1 John 2:27
I believe God for healing.	I have the healing and I am the healing. Isaiah 53:5

I cry for the outpouring of the Spirit.	The Spirit has been poured out to me. Acts 2:4
I always wait for God to speak and hear His voice from Heaven.	God has already spoken to us though His Son. Hebrews 1:2
I try to earn my healing.	Christ has already paid for my healing. 1 Peter 2:24
When I do something bad then God is angry at me.	God will never be angry at me ever again. Isaiah 54:9
I suffer because of the generational curse.	We have been redeemed from the curse. Galatians 3:14-15
I am always asking for the favor from God.	I have God's favor and it doesn't leave me.
I am seeking for God's presence.	I am the temple of the Holy Spirit. 1 Corinthians 6:19
I am seeking and chasing God's glory.	I am the very glory of God. Colossians 1:27
I am fighting for victory.	I am more than conqueror in Christ Jesus. Romans 8:35
I boast on how I love God.	I focus on how God loves me. 1 John 3:1; 4:19

A New Covenant mentality is focused on the person and not on the process. It is defined by relationship and not by rules and regulations. It is not about begging but believing. It is not about do, do, do, but about a *done* deal. It is all about the finished work and the person of Jesus Christ.

III. The New Covenant Message: Interpretation

The Bible is God's love letter towards us, not a bunch of rules and regulations. A love letter is a letter that contains words of love and admiration. Imagine if I wrote my wife, Rucelle, a love letter that demands and pressures her to be someone I wanted her to become. I bet she wouldn't like it, and instead of treasuring it, she would probably rip it up and throw it on the floor. The Scriptures are God's revelation of who He is, and His message for all of us. It contains a message of love, grace and mercy; a message from God the Father that is encapsulated by, and in, His Son, Jesus Christ.

We read and interpret Scripture through the lenses of the Cross and the New Covenant. It should be read according to the promise given about Jesus Christ; His birth, His life, His obedience, His death, His resurrection and His second coming.

> "God, who at various times and in various ways spoke in time past to the fathers by the prophets, has in these last days spoken to us by His Son, whom He has appointed heir of all things,"
>
> \- Hebrews 1:1-3 (NKJV)

There are some keys to interpreting Scripture correctly.

A. The Context

Who wrote it, why was it written, to whom was it written? What was the author's purpose and why did he write it? Does the audience consist of Hebrews, Jews, Gentiles? Is it a personal letter or a letter for the Church?

Paul Ellis writes on his blog, *Escape to Reality* [1], that there are only two kinds of people – those who put their faith in Jesus and those who don't. Consequently, the Holy Spirit brings two different convictions:

1. Jesus said the Holy Spirit would convict the world of guilt for the sin of unbelief (John 16:9). Many things in the New Testament are written for unbelievers. Paul, Peter, John, Jude, and James all had things to say to those who did not see their need for a Savior (e.g. 1 John 1:5-10). The apostles also wrote to warn the Church about sinners masquerading as prophets and preachers (e.g. 2 Peter 2). Strong words of judgment and condemnation given to sinners do not apply to those whom Christ has qualified.

2. Jesus also said the Holy Spirit would convict Christians of righteousness (John 16:10). We do not need to be reminded of our shortcomings, but we often need to be reminded of our right standing before God (2 Corinthians 5:21). Much of the New Testament was written to assure Christians that we belong to God, and that nothing can separate us from the love of Christ (Romans 8:38-39). Not even our sin can separate us because God's grace is greater than our sin (Romans 5:15). When we fail, the Holy Spirit does not condemn us – there is no condemnation to those in Christ. Rather, He reminds us that we are righteous, that we are kept by Jesus (Jude 24), that we are the Father's sons (Galatians 4:6), and that our hope is firm and secure (Hebrews 6:19). When we make mistakes Jesus doesn't condemn us, He defends us (1 John 2:1) and then He teaches us how to say no to ungodliness (Titus 2:12).

B. The Cross

Is the passage, story and situation rendered and read before or after the

Cross? Is it before the death and resurrection of Jesus Christ? Many believers know the importance of context but do not know the difference between a before or after the Cross truth.

- Before the Cross, blessings are earned. After the Cross, blessings are gifts of undeserved favor.
- Before the Cross, forgiveness is given as we forgive others (Matthew 6:14-15, *"For if you forgive men their trespasses, your heavenly Father will also forgive you. But if you do not forgive men their trespasses, neither will your Father forgive your trespasses.")*. After the Cross, we can forgive because the Lord has already forgiven us (Colossians 3:13).
- Before the Cross righteousness is demanded. After the Cross, righteousness is a gift.
- Before the Cross it's a ministry of death. After the Cross, it is a ministry of life.
- Before the Cross, obedience is a key to blessings. After the Cross, obedience is the by-product of favor.
- Before the Cross, "*Cursed is every one that does not continue in all things which are written in the book of the law.*" After the Cross, "*Blessed is the man whose iniquities are forgiven, whose sin is taken away; blessed is the man to whom the Lord will not impute iniquity.*"
- Before the Cross, "*You shall love the Lord your God with all your heart, and with all your mind, and with all your strength.*" After the Cross, "*Here is love; not that we love God, but He loved us, and sent His Son to be the propitiation for our sins.*"

C. The Covenant

Does the scripture fall under the Old Covenant or the New Covenant?

What is the relationship of the text, story, and passage to the New Covenant of grace? Is it under the Abrahamic Covenant which is based on lineage? Is it under Mosaic Covenant which is based on law, performance, human effort, and behavior, or is it under the New Covenant which is pure love, grace, faith, and sonship?

The Old Covenant is focused on human effort, whereas the New Covenant is focused on God's effort. Everything that doesn't have its source in God is a work of the flesh, and it is opposed to the covenant of the Spirit.

Effort is not bad, but it becomes bad when we get our approval because of it. When we don't consider God as our source, then we rely on human effort and human strength.

Origen said the following,

> "I do not call the Law an 'Old Testament' if I understand it in the Spirit. The Law becomes an 'Old Testament' only for those who understand it carnally, but for those who understand it and apply it in the Spirit and in the Gospel sense, the Law is ever new and the two Testaments are new Testaments for us, not because of their date in time but because of the newness of the meaning. For those who do not respect the covenant of love, even the Gospels are 'old'."

You can read the Scriptures from a perspective of the Old or the New Covenant. Any part of the Bible becomes a New Covenant truth when it is read in the light and through the lenses of grace, which is the loveliness of Jesus' person and His finished work.

A New Covenant man is a man who knows the significance of blessing and happiness, his mind is inclined to Jesus and he stands in the truth of Scripture, not by the deception of traditions, destruction of the law, or destitution of religion. He knows the power of the Cross and the loveliness of Jesus Christ and His finished work. The New Covenant man knows that he has the nature of Christ, his mentality is the 'norm of the Cross' and his message is the New Covenant.

Jesus is the center and the solid ground in which we all stand, He is the word of God who became flesh (John 1:14). He is the way, the truth and life (John 14:6). He is our wisdom, sanctification, righteousness and redemption (1 Corinthians 1:30). He is our, "Yes and Amen," (2 Corinthians 1:20). He is the name above all names (Acts 4:12). He is the light of the world (John 8:12), the living water (John 4:10), the bread of life (John 6:35,48). He is the I Am (John 14:6), the Author and finisher of our faith (Hebrews 12:2). Before Abraham, He Is (John 8:58). He is Jesus Christ, the darling of Heaven, the center of everything, He is the person of grace.

Endnotes

1. "Rightly Dividing The Word: How To Read Your Bible Without Getting Confused." Escape to Reality Blog (http://escapetoreality.org/2010/03/10/rightly-dividing-the-word-how-to-read-your-bible-without-getting-confused/)

Chapter 12

New Covenant Motivation

by Wayne Duncan

Why Do We Do the Things That We Do?

Will God punish you when you sin?

Will God pour out His wrath on you when you sin?

Will you be separated from God when you sin?

Will the Holy Spirit leave you when you sin?

Will you lose your salvation when you sin?

Does God stop loving you when you sin?

The answer to all of these questions is a resounding, NO!

The good news of the New Covenant is that Jesus bore the punishment of our sin, in Himself, on the Cross. So the question arises, "Shall we just continue in sin?"

This has always been the great attack against grace.

The accusation, "If you preach grace, people will just go out and sin more."

The answer, "*Grace teaches us to say no to sin,*" and, "*Sin shall not have dominion over you, for you are not under law but under grace,*" and, "New creation spirits do not want to sin."

At the heart of all this, are these fundamental questions:

"Why do we do the things that we do?"

And,

"How do we motivate each other in the New Covenant?"

The simple truth is that it is good to define and encourage good behavior. This does not mean you are putting people under the law. The law says when you sin, you will be punished, you will be separated from God, you will lose your fruit of the Holy Spirit, you will lose your salvation and God will stop loving you. Once grace brings freedom from the fear and the threat of punishment, all motivational factors change. We can freely model and teach a godly lifestyle, knowing that the power of sin, failure and condemnation is broken.

Jesus did not assign us to simply bear fruit. Merely having some fruit does not mean we are living the abundant life that Jesus gives. We are called to so much more.

> "By this my Father is glorified, that you bear much fruit and so prove to be my disciples."
>
> - John 15:8 (ESV)

Here we see that Father is glorified by us bearing *much* fruit. I believe that the key to much fruit is found just three verses before this, in verse 5:

> "I am the vine; you are the branches. Whoever abides in me and I in him, he it is that bears much fruit, for apart from me you can do nothing."
>
> - John 15:5 (ESV)

Much fruit comes from knowing that we can do nothing apart from Him, and by abiding in Him.

"Abide in me." This statement by Jesus speaks of relationship and sustainability.

Here, in South Africa, there is a lot of hype around the word "sustainability". Because of more than a decade of transformation from the Old

South Africa to the New, this word has much relevance in our land. The basic idea is that many policies and plans come along that seem good and relevant and promise great things, however, while many of these projects often have good short term results, in the long term, the project becomes a failure. Why? The policies and plans that drive those initiatives cannot be sustained! Sustainability is a very relevant topic for believers. Many have a short burst of fruitfulness, but Jesus wants fruit that abides and lasts. Abiding is sustaining.

Working from a Place of Rest

Working from rest does not speak of passivity, but rather active duty from a place of rest. This rest comes from knowing our identity and security. It's important to know this. The ultimate goal of working from a place of rest is not passivity, but resting from dead works. It is based on a revelation that we are righteous because of a gift of God's grace. We do not work to become accepted, we do not work to gain approval, we do not work to get love. We have ceased from working for those things. We have approval, love, favor, blessing, acceptance and "every spiritual blessing".

The Bible calls us *to* "good works," and *away from* "dead works".

The Call to "Good Works"

"For we are his workmanship, created in Christ Jesus for good works, which God prepared beforehand, that we should walk in them."

- Ephesians 2:10 (ESV)

> "Therefore let us leave the elementary doctrine of Christ and go on to maturity, not laying again a foundation of repentance from dead works and of faith toward God,"
>
> - Hebrews 6:1 (ESV)

It's interesting to note that one of the Christian foundations is repentance from dead works.

Notice the link between faith and repentance from dead works, here it is again.

> "[1] Therefore, while the promise of entering his rest still stands, let us fear lest any of you should seem to have failed to reach it. [2] For good news came to us just as to them, but the message they heard did not benefit them, because they were not united by faith with those who listened. [3] For we who have believed enter that rest....[9] So then, there remains a Sabbath rest for the people of God, [10] for whoever has entered God's rest has also rested from his works as God did from his. [11] Let us therefore strive to enter that rest, so that no one may fall by the same sort of disobedience."
>
> - Hebrews 4 (ESV)

These passages clearly show that we should repent from dead works by adding our faith to the Gospel message. Understanding the difference between "dead works" and "good works" is essential. How do we distinguish between "good works" and "dead works?"

It comes down to motivation. *Why do we do the things that we do?*

There are various motivational factors that operate in believers' lives. We will look at a few and examine essential components of each type of motivation.

We will look at the relational aspect (with God and others). We will look at the faith aspect, and we will look at sustainability. Remember that Jesus wanted us to produce fruit, and much fruit, by abiding in Him. This must all be considered in evaluating the strengths and weaknesses of each motivational factor.

There are four major motivational factors: fear, reward, faith and love.

Motivation by Fear

There is no doubt that fear is a powerful motivator. Fear can drive people to do things, and fear can stop people from doing things. The problem that I see concerning motivation by fear, is a relational one. What kind of relationship do you have with someone you fear? Would you abide in them?

At the age of about ten, while I was in primary school, one our subjects was Afrikaans, one of the two official languages in South Africa at the time. I remember my Afrikaans teacher very well. She was very strict, and we were all terrified of her. She would punish us harshly for anything and everything we did wrong. If we talked in class, she would make us stand outside the class for the whole lesson, or stand at the front of the class. She would shout at us, and if we had the wrong answers in our work, she would pull our hair and ears. If we did badly in our speeches or exams, she would take us into the room at the back of the classroom, get us to bend over and spank us with a wooden plank.

One day, I remember having to memorize a poem. Man, I was so scared of the punishment. I learned that poem perfectly. I knew every word, my mom tested me and I did it perfectly every time.

The next day at class, when my turn came to recite the poem, I was so scared and nervous that I totally messed it up. I mixed up lines and pronounced words wrong. Fear made me do badly. Yes, I did get a visit to the back room that day. It was the first time anyone besides my parents had given me a hiding.

My relationship with that teacher was very bad. Did I fear her? Yes. Did it help me? No.

What do you think was the fruit of my relationship with that teacher? How do you think I enjoyed using and speaking in Afrikaans? The relationship had such a big impact on my experience of Afrikaans that, even though I was barely 11 years old, at the end of the year I took all my books, put them in a wheelbarrow, and burned them. No sustainability.

Fear Has Flaws

Jesus said that much fruit comes from abiding in Him. Does fear produce abiding; a strong, solid relationship?

Where did man first fear God? In the relationship between the Creator and the creation, *when* was fear introduced in the relationship? *Who* introduced it, and *how* was it introduced?

To discover this we need to journey way back, in fact, all the way to the Garden of Eden.

> "[8] And they heard the sound of the LORD God walking in the garden in the cool of the day, and the man and his wife hid themselves from the presence of the LORD God among the trees of the garden. [9] But the LORD God called to the man and said to him, 'Where are you?'[10] And he said, 'I heard the sound of you in the garden, and I was afraid, because I was naked, and I hid myself."
>
> - Genesis 3:8-10 (ESV)

Here we find that when Adam and Eve ate of the Tree of the Knowledge of Good and Evil, they became afraid. This is where fear was introduced into the relationship between Creator and creation, at the Fall.

God had given Adam and Eve a mandate to be fruitful and to multiply, but when fear was introduced, they became unfruitful and hid from God. You cannot be fruitful while you are in hiding! You are not abiding when you are hiding. Fear is part of the Fall. God did not demand it, He did not ask for it or insist on it in the original Adamic Covenant. Fear came through knowledge of good and evil, fuelled by an uncertainty of how God would react to their disobedience.

Before fear and the knowledge of good and evil, Adam and Eve would walk and talk with God in the cool of the day. That's abiding. They were fruitful and reigning in authority.

They were abiding, and bearing much fruit, but through the Fall, that intimacy was disrupted. Fear was part of that disruption in relationship.

It's interesting to me that Adam was not commanded to fear God. Fear was not part of the motivation that God gave Adam in the garden. God was content to create a perfect environment, an environment that God and man was well pleased with. Man was placed into this environment and given an assignment. God did not introduce fear into this perfect environment, it came by the knowledge of good and evil.

Jesus came to bring us into a relationship where we can serve God without fear.

In Luke 1, we see John's father prophesying over John about how he would prepare the way for the one who would bring salvation, and fulfill the covenant God swore to Abraham. In this prophecy, Zechariah says the Messiah would, "*enable us to serve Him without fear*".

> "[67] His father Zechariah was filled with the Holy Spirit and prophesied: [68] 'Praise be to the Lord, the God of Israel, because he has come and has redeemed his people. [69] He has raised up a horn of salvation for us in the house of his servant David [70] (as he said through his holy prophets of long ago), [71] salvation from our enemies and from the hand of all who hate us – [72] to show mercy to our fathers and to remember his holy covenant, [73] the oath he swore to our father Abraham: [74] to rescue us from the hand of our enemies, and to enable us to serve him without fear [75] in holiness and righteousness before him all our days.'"
>
> - Luke 1:67-75 (NIV)

This is a very powerful statement. The Old Covenant was fear based. Jesus came to remove the fear factor.

> "There is no fear in love, but perfect love casts out fear. For fear has to do with punishment, and whoever fears has not been perfected in love."
>
> - 1 John 4:18 (NIV)

Here we see that love actually casts out fear, and that fear has to do with punishment. This is a very important scripture when it comes to motivating Christian behavior.

"Fear God and serve Him, and if you don't, He will punish you."

This is the language of fear motivation. It is an Old Covenant mindset, which can be totally neutralized by understanding the atonement and the finished work of the Cross. In the New Covenant, there is no punishment from God for the believer who sins. Jesus was our propitiating sacrifice. The punishment that we deserved, fell on Him. This is a powerful truth that I deal with comprehensively in my book *A Matter of Life and Death*. In brief, one of the clauses of the New Covenant is that God will not count our sins against us. We will, therefore, never be punished for our sin. Jesus was punished for our sin, and God will not punish us.

Once you know this, fear as a motivator will lose a lot of its power in your life.

It's important to note that although God will never punish you, there are still consequences to sin. Jail, a criminal record, heartache, loss of finances, family stress, marriage disruption, bad health, damaged relationships with children, loss of ministry integrity, and opening a door to the enemy, are all consequences of sin. We can also lose our peace, our feeling of righteousness, and our joy, by running away from God's way, but it is never God punishing you when these things happen.

Now, when we realize that when we are abiding we simply sin less, and when we fear, we hide and sin more; it becomes obvious that fear is very unhelpful in producing a life that is marked with much fruit.

One area where motivation is needed in the Church, is in the area of ministering in individual gifting. In order for a church to function well, you need many people using the gifting that they have. It's interesting to note that in the parable of the talents in Matthew 25, two people were fruitful, they were motivated and producing fruit, but the third was not fruitful. What was the difference between the three people? One of the major differences was their perception of their master. Notice here what the unfruitful servant said:

> "[24] He also who had received the one talent came forward, saying, 'Master, I knew you to be a hard man, reaping where you did not sow, and gathering where you scattered no seed, [25] so I was afraid, and I went and hid your talent in the ground."
>
> - Matthew 25:24-25 (ESV)

It is interesting to me that the one which feared God hid the money and he produced the least fruit! Fear caused him not only to hide himself, but his gift also.

So Is There Any Value in Fearing God?

Well, fearing God can have a restraining effect when it comes to sinning less.

> "Through love and faithfulness sin is atoned for; through the fear of the LORD a man avoids evil."
>
> - Proverbs 16:6 (NIV)

> "By steadfast love and faithfulness iniquity is atoned for, and by the fear of the LORD one turns away from evil."
>
> - Proverbs 16:6 (ESV)

So here we see fear producing a turning away from evil, or as the NIV says, "avoiding evil". This is obviously a good thing. But notice that it mentions here a superior way. The way of love. It produces atonement or purging. Fear turns away, or avoids. Love, however, changes the person from the inside out, and this has a purging effect.

> Purge - To cleanse, clear, or purify by separating and carrying off whatever is impure, heterogeneous, foreign, or superfluous.
>
> - Webster's Biblical Dictionary

Purging is a very powerful thing. Purging is what happens when all of an unwanted substance is being removed. Purging purifies, it removes every poison. A body purged of poison has no trace of the poison left in it.

Fear has effect on a single event at a time, purging affects everything, at every level. This is a new creation, Holy Spirit reality. Thus we see that although there is some value in fear, it is an inferior motivator, with partial, unsustainable results.

How many times do you think we are commanded to fear God in the New Testament?

Do you know that it appears only once? This does not mean we can ignore this scripture, for all of the Word is true. It does, however, show that this is not the *dominant* New Testament means to motivate purity or good works.

It is always good to revere God, He is the Creator, He will judge the living and the dead. We will all stand before Him and give an account for our lives. He is majestic, He is powerful, He is above all. Everyone who has ever seen Him has fallen down in fear, and everyone who ever fell down before Him was immediately told, "Fear not."

When you read the New Testament, one does not get the impression that we should approach His throne with fear. Instead, we have the parable of the prodigal son, where the father runs to his returning son, kissing him and hugging him. We are encouraged to call God, Father. We are told that we are God's friend, His throne is called the throne of "mercy and grace". We are taught to be confident, to boldly enter. This is the dominant encouragement of the New Testament teaching and writings. We call Him "Abba"; Daddy, Father.

It's in this place, and by abiding in this place, that we produce much fruit and good fruit.

Fear God and Keep His Law

I would like to say that I believe that we should always obey God. Always!

But the reason is not that we fear Him. That mentality is a legalistic mentality. It is based on the old way of the letter, and not on the heart which is the new way of the spirit (2 Corinthians 3).

It's interesting to me that biblically, we had to be released from the law in order to bear fruit to God. Romans 7 is so clear here.

> "[4] Likewise, my brothers, you also have died to the law through the body of Christ, so that you may belong to another, to him who has been raised from the dead, in order that we may bear fruit for God. [5] For while we were living in the flesh, our sinful passions, aroused by the law, were at work in our members to bear fruit for death. [6] But now we are released from the law, having died to that which held us captive, so that we serve not under the old written code but in the new life of the Spirit."
>
> - Romans 7:4-6 (ESV)

We had to die to the law *in order* that we might bear fruit to God.

The law only aroused sin, and we are released from the law *so that*, we can serve in the *new way of the spirit.*

So here we see a correlation between law and fruit. We died to the law, in order to belong to another, so that we may bear fruit to God. Under the Law we bear fruit for death.

The reason is that the Law is a ministry of condemnation. Where there is condemnation, there is no abiding. Condemnation only causes hiding. Through Jesus, we were reconciled to the Father, so that we might bear fruit.

As a motivating factor in a Christian's life, fear is ,therefore, an inferior motive filled with danger and pitfalls. A life that has fear as the dominant influence, could not produce the abiding, and therefore, the much fruit, that Jesus spoke of.

Motivation by Reward

Leaving fear behind, we move now to another motivating factor.

Are we to be rewarded for our good works, our holiness and service?

Will we be rewarded in this life? Will we be rewarded in the life to come?

Are There Rewards in This Life?

If we plant a seed, or water a seed, or harvest a crop, is there not a reward? If we sow the Word into someone's life and it is received, is there not great joy? When we show love and kindness to someone and they are comforted, are we not ourselves comforted? When we teach and share revelation with someone, and they 'see it', are we ourselves not encouraged? When we sow seeds of finance, and it returns with a harvest, are we not blessed? When we pray for someone, and we see a miracle, are we not uplifted? When we are faithful with the little, and we are given more, are we not encouraged? When we invest time and effort into relationships, are we not blessed by those friendships? What farmer sows a seed and expects no share in the harvest?

We are indeed rewarded in this life for the good things we do.

We receive increase, joy, peace, encouragement, and many other rewards, for doing good works and for living pure lives. The beautiful thing about these rewards is that they are fully available to everyone, all the time!

By His grace, we can do good works and live pure lives. By His grace, He has blessed us in the heavenly realms with every blessing in Christ, His divine power is at work in our lives, and He works in us to act and to will according to His good purpose. By His grace he has filled every one of us with His Holy Spirit, and united us to Himself. His grace has placed the fruit of the spirit in us; it makes us partakers of His divine nature. It's His grace that produces every good thing in us. When all this bursts out of us, then we are blessed all the more by watching the power of it work, and it is very rewarding.

There is a great personal reward in this life for living godly lives and serving God and others.

We have more joy, more peace, better relationships, better social standing, broken addictions and bad habits... the rewards go on and on.

What About Eternal Rewards?

One day we will stand before God, and our good works will be judged, and we will be praised and rewarded for the good things done on Earth. Now you may not agree with me here, and that is fine, but let me explain what I believe about the future.

There will be a new Heaven and a new Earth. Satan and all his power and influence will be removed. Death will be destroyed, all sickness and pain and suffering will be gone. We will then rule and reign with Jesus on the new Earth. We will be assigned eternal positions in that eternal perfect kingdom, where we will work and live with God. Our positions and activities will be part of the reward for being good stewards of what we had on Earth. The way we use our lives here has eternal relevance.

However, the fact that we have different roles and positions in Heaven

does not mean that there will be different degrees of joy, peace, and satisfaction. We will all be totally satisfied by God and the glory of His presence.

Another aspect of eternal reward, is that you will see the people in Heaven, that you helped get there! That's an eternal reward! So yes, there are eternal rewards, and it is good to live with that eternal perspective.

This has value to help us see that we are not living only for the here and now, but for eternity, and with eternity in our hearts. A person who would like to see people saved so that those who get saved can enjoy eternity with God, is well motivated, and will receive an eternal reward.

When we realize that our gifting, service, obedience, and fellowship all work together to redeem a lost world by encouraging other Christians and equipping other Christians for service, we are positively motivated, having an eternal mindset.

Jesus did encourage this kind of thinking when He spoke about, "laying up for yourselves treasures in Heaven, where moth and rust cannot destroy, and where thieves cannot break in and steal." Jesus said, "Where your heart is, there your treasure will be," if we set our hearts on Heaven, we will lay up treasures there.

Living with this mentality is a good motivator to good deeds, and even purity.

We want to live lives that are attractive to the lost so that they will turn to Jesus. Many have been saved through looking at a Christian and saying, "I want what they've got!"

If a Christian is a drug addict, broken in body and in spirit, still living in blatant ongoing sin, hurting people, not caring about anyone else, and totally selfish, this does not bring glory to God. They are still the righteousness of Christ, just not living in a righteous way. My point here is that a person like that is not a good representation of the Gospel. The Gospel brings freedom from addiction and strongholds and sin. This is what the lost want. Deep down, the lost want addictions broken and the power of sin destroyed. They want happy, whole and healed lives.

When we allow the Gospel to do that to us, we become a pleasant aroma in the world, the aroma of Christ, and the world will want what we have. We shine like stars in a perverse and crooked generation. If people are attracted to the Gospel through your fragrance, they will turn to Christ, this is a reward in itself, in this world and in eternity.

We should always be careful that we are not seeking these rewards in a totally selfish way. We could seek reward so much that we lose sight of the fact that our reward is in seeing *others* blessed. In this way we end up seeking only to bless ourselves, and we build for, and towards, ourselves. The goal is always to see others come into eternity, and for others to know Him.

If we share the Gospel with someone because we want them to be in Heaven for eternity, that is pure, but when we share the Gospel so we can feel good about ourselves, we miss the point of this reward.

We will see those who we lead to the Lord in Heaven, and it will be a great reward. But the greatest reward is that *they* are in Heaven, not that we feel good for eternity because of it.

So there are rewards in this life and in the life to come... this is all by grace. All this is available and possible only because of the Gospel of Grace. It's because of what God has given us in the finished work, and it is because we are regenerated new creations, united to God, filled with His Spirit and made partakers in His divine nature. We want good things for

others, for we share in the nature of God.

The Excellent Way

Now I would like to come to what I consider to be the perfect motivator.

There are no cautions to this motivator. There are no pitfalls. There need be no balance or guidelines established. It is the most powerful motivator, the most pure, the most effective. This has the ability to produce much fruit, sustainably. It upholds Jesus' call to abide.

It is superior by far to fear, and completes rewards.

The New Covenant motivation, through the finished work of the Cross, is:

Love expressing itself through faith.

We love and we believe, and therefore, we do. Jesus said that all the law and the commandments hang on love, and that love fulfils the law.

Love is powerful! Wars have been fought for love. People have crossed oceans, gone without, exerted great energy, worked, given money and done anything and everything else you could possibly think of...for love.

Love changes the way you think, it changes the way you feel.

The power of love is that it produces a purity about what you do; a purity that flows from a heartfelt devotion. A pure motive is a heart issue. Here is a definition that I will suggest for Christian purity:

Purity: Christian behavior that flows from nothing but un-manipulated love.

This is pure and powerful.

Did you notice that I said un-manipulated? That's important.

Once love is manipulated it loses its purity. If we lose our purity in motivation, it means that we are not keeping love for others and love for the Lord as the central motivational factor.

Motivation by love loses its purity when people can hold love over you as a whip, and demand more service or obedience.

What do I mean by that?

Consider these statements.

"If you love God, prove it by giving the church more money."

"If you love God, you should be more obedient."

"If you love God, you should treat other Christians better."

"If you love God, you should serve more."

"If you love God, you should evangelize more."

Now none of these statements are wrong, but if a person were to give money to the church to prove they love God, they have been manipulated, and the motivation is not pure.

If you evangelize out of obedience, to prove your love of people and your devotion to God, you lose purity.

All of the things that flow from a Christian life can be sustained, and continually motivated, if love could arrest our hearts.

It's not about proving anything or earning anything. If this is the motivation, well then it is a dead work.

Faith expressing itself through love:

I believe that this Gospel is indeed very good news. I have to share it with you. I truly love you, God loves you, and with all my heart I hope that you will receive this good news.

Faith expressing itself through love:

This Gospel is the only hope for the lost world. It takes money to reach the world. I gladly give my finances, time and life to see people changed and brought into this Gospel.

Faith expressing itself through love:

I believe I can do all things through Him who strengthens me. I know God loves me, I love myself. He does not want me to have this sin pattern in my life. It is broken through the power of Jesus.

Faith expressing itself through love:

Believers will lay hands on the sick and they shall recover. All the things that Jesus did, I can do too, and greater. I love you, God loves you, and so I want to pray for you to be healed right now.

This is powerful pure motivation.

This comes from abiding, and it will bear much fruit.

There is no earning, no working, no dead works, no manipulation...it is the perfect way.

Love and Holiness, Love and Relationships

"[12] Put on then, as God's chosen ones, holy and beloved, compassion, kindness, humility, meekness, and patience, [13] bearing with one another and, if one has a complaint against another, forgiving each

> other; as the Lord has forgiven you, so you also must forgive. [14] And above all these put on love, which binds everything together in perfect harmony.
>
> - Colossians 3:12-14 (NIV)

Did you notice "*And above all these put on love, which binds everything together in perfect harmony*"?

Here it says, "*above all these*". If you can get love above all these, then all the other things will fall into place.

Put on love, and holiness, compassion, kindness, humility, meekness, patience, bearing with each other, forgiveness… all these things will be bound together. Love has the power to affect multiple levels of our lives.

Practically, if you love someone you will not murder them. If you love God, you will worship no other. You don't need to be told to treat someone you love well.

I love this; "*Forgive one another as the Lord has forgiven you.*"

How has God forgiven us?

He has forgiven us all our sins, completely, in advance, with no strings attached, for He loves us.

Imagine doing the same for each other, imagine the power of it!

Imagine not being able to hold a grudge, because the government of love for that person is just too great! Imagine when someone says, "Please forgive me," you could respond, "I already have, totally and completely."

Love is the government of Heaven.

Love in Ministry, Gifting and Service

[27] Now you are the body of Christ and individually members of it. [28] And God has appointed in the church first apostles, second prophets, third teachers, then miracles, then gifts of healing, helping, administrating, and various kinds of tongues. [29] Are all apostles? Are all prophets? Are all teachers? Do all work miracles? [30] Do all possess gifts of healing? Do all speak with tongues? Do all interpret? [31] But earnestly desire the higher gifts. And I will show you a still more excellent way:

[1] If I speak in the tongues of men and of angels, but have not love, I am a noisy gong or a clanging cymbal. [2] And if I have prophetic powers, and understand all mysteries and all knowledge, and if I have all faith, so as to remove mountains, but have not love, I am nothing. [3] If I give away all I have, and if I deliver up my body to be burned, but have not love, I gain nothing.

- 1 Corinthians 12:27 – 13:3 (ESV)

This is a staggering scripture which reveals a lot about love.

Here we see that the work of the apostle; the prophet; teachers; miracle workers; healings; helping; administrating, and the gifts of the spirit...if not done in love, are just a clanging symbol.

If you use gifts to show off, or to seem important, or with an ambitious motive, or out of insecurity…clang, clang, the motive is not love, and the purity of love is again lost.

That means no matter how powerful or prominent an apostle is, how wonderful the movement seems, if there is not love…clang clang!

If you can prophesy with accuracy, and see many wonderful things, if there is no love...clang clang.

If you can teach the deepest truths, and have the deepest revelation, but no love…clang clang.

If you are highly gifted, but have not love. If you understand mysteries and have knowledge, if you have faith and do great things, if you are loyal to the point of death, if you give everything but have no love, you gain nothing. It is all…clang clang.

You can perfectly administrate what you do, it can run smoothly and be super slick, but without love…clang clang.

This passage should convince us of the great need to have everything we do rooted and grounded in love.

This means that the state of the heart is more important than the activity itself.

After all, if the motive is not love, what is the motive?

It must be self: Self promotion, self preservation, self righteousness.

God does not see as we do. We always look at the surface, at the activity, at the observable results. God however, looks at the heart.

What Motivated God to Send Jesus?

"for God so loved…that he sent…"

- John 3:16

This makes teaching people about the love of God of utmost importance. Our love for God is in direct proportion to the revelation that we have of how much He loves us, a love reflected and revealed in the Cross. We love, for He first loves us. Remember the parable of the man who was forgiven much? Jesus said, "The one who is forgiven much, loves much."

> [9] In this the love of God was made manifest among us, that God sent his only Son into the world, so that we might live through him. [10] In this is love, not that we have loved God but that he loved us and sent his Son to be the propitiation for our sins.
>
> - 1 John 4:9-10 (ESV)

This means that in the Gospel message is contained the heart of God, a heart of love. How do we know what love looks like? By understanding the Gospel.

The Gospel reveals the nature and character of God; gracious, compassionate, slow to anger and abounding in love. Did you notice God's motivation in sending His son? It is love!

Do you see why God wants us to have life?

Love!

Why did Christ become our sin? Why did Christ absorb God's wrath against us? Why did Jesus pay the price for our sin and union with God?

Love!

God is pure...His motives flow always and only from love.

God is love!

Knowledge

The other essential component for living a well motivated life is knowledge. Every believer simply needs to know the Word. Here we discover the Gospel; God's plan to redeem a lost world in love. Here we learn our authority; here we learn who we are in Christ. Here we learn what the promises are. All this knowledge works to strengthen us, and ultimately motivate us.

Faith is about believing. Knowledge tells us what to believe.

How do we know we have authority over the enemy? How do we know we can heal the sick? How do we know what the Gospel is? How do we know God loves us? How will we tell the love story, with all its wonderful benefits, if we do not know the story, or the benefits? How will we live in the promise if we don't know what it is?

When we know how good the Gospel is, we will be well motivated to shout it to the world!

You Can do Abundantly More Through Love

Look at this powerful prayer Paul prayed for the Church:

> 14 For this reason I bow my knees before the Father, 15 from whom every family in heaven and on earth is named, 16 that according to the riches of his glory he may grant you to be strengthened with power through his Spirit in your inner being, 17 so that Christ may dwell in your hearts through faith – that you, being rooted and grounded in love, 18 may have strength to comprehend with all the saints what is the breadth and length and height and depth, 19 and to know the love of Christ that surpasses knowledge, that you may be filled with all the fullness of God. 20 Now to him who is able to do far more abundantly than all that we ask or think, according to the power at work within us.
>
> - Ephesians 3:14-20 (ESV)

He calls God, Father. He speaks about the strengthening through His Spirit, about Christ in us by faith, about being rooted and grounded in love, to comprehend the greatness of God's love, to be filled with all the fullness.

Then Paul says, "*Now*". Did you see it?

Only after we have all that in place, once these things, including the love of God, are rooted and grounded, do we come to the doing abundantly part. Rooted and grounded implies steadiness, consistency, depth. When a plant is rooted and grounded well, you know that with nourishment, good fruit will come!

We have been given these things, freely by grace, in love. If we will receive it, believe it, be rooted and grounded in it...then we can live a life of abundantly more than all we ask, think or imagine. That is abiding, and that is much fruit.

This is a well motivated son of God, bearing much fruit.

CHAPTER 13

Unstoppable Grace

by Lucas Miles

Hopefully, by now, it is clear to you that *The Living Grace Project* isn't really this book, or merely ink on a page – rather, The Living Grace Project is you. It's all of us – the whole world. As Paul writes, "*The creation waits in eager expectation for the sons of God to be revealed*" (Romans 8:19). We are, as Paul pens to the Ephesians, "*God's workmanship, created in Christ Jesus to do good works, which God prepared in advance for us to do.*" This 'living grace' works in us, moves in us, and transforms us into His image. We are the blessed recipients of His love and affection.

This grace that has brought us all together, that has set us free, that has transformed us into His image, that has elevated us, that has removed every barrier to the throne of God and imparted His righteousness unto us, is not just for us, but for people everywhere. They too, as 'living grace projects', are eagerly awaiting their transformation through faith in Christ. We possess in our grasp the message, and most of all, the One – the one the world is looking for, the one who can make a man whole – the person Jesus Christ. This grace that we share in is too precious for us to keep to ourselves. Let us in grace, by grace, and through grace, strive to take the message of our redemption to this broken world, so that all might know Him and find their hope in Him. Thankfully, this is exactly what is taking place.

All Over the World

As the President of a global grace-based church planting organization called *The Oasis Network For Churches* (www.oasnet.org), I've had the privilege of working with countless men and women who are on the front lines of world evangelism and church development. Specifically, this past year in East Africa, one of our network pastors spoke about the finished work of Christ and the message of grace at a large church leader's conference just outside of Nairobi. Afterwards, the head of the pastor's association came to him and confessed that until he heard this message, none of those attending had known that salvation was by grace, and not law. This man went on to tell our pastor that because of this testimony, that all 250 of those present at the conference made a pact to only preach salvation by grace through faith, and to remove the burden of the law from their own congregations! I have received countless stories like this one from places like St. Lucia, Malaysia, Canada, and the United States. In fact, even as I write this, we are working on a ground breaking church plant in South Sudan, a nation which is only a few months old. I can't even begin to tell you how exciting and rewarding it has been to witness the birth of this global gospel reformation.

For the first time in centuries, the Church is coming to embrace the goodness of God, the finished work of the Cross, and the power of the Holy Spirit. Grace is no longer just a synonym for prayer, but a meaningful description of God's favor and transforming work in our life through the person of Christ. Through this understanding of who He is and who we are in Him, the Church is being set free from years of religious traditions, poor interpretations of Scripture, and needless efforts attempting to get God to love us.

All over the world, the Church is in fervent expectation for the coming change. This revolution will come not with sticks and clubs, but with the message of God's grace – the Gospel of Jesus Christ. As a friend of mine once put it (referring to the coming grace revolution), *"The main difference between a rebel and a revolutionary is this - a rebel fights because of what he stands against, but a revolutionary fights because of what he stands for."* I couldn't agree more. Today, the fight driving the gospel revolution is not about being *against* the law, but it's about being *for* the revelation of Jesus Christ. With this spirit in mind, the stage has been set. Missionary efforts and global church planting are at an all time high and the Gospel is going forth with power. With the boom of the Internet and mobile broadband, for the first time ever we now have the resources and the technological platforms to fulfill the Great Commission – to reach every nation for Christ. I believe that we stand on the brink of the greatest awakening the Church or this world has ever seen.

But as the Gospel of Grace rises up, so do its enemies. Enemies which attempt to thwart the plans of God. Yet, as we see time and time again, persecution cannot stop what God has started. Even in recent news, an Iranian pastor, Youcef Nadarkhani was sentenced to death by a regional court in Rasht, the largest city on Iran's northern coast, accused of apostasy against Islam. According to *The Voice of the Martyrs*, one of the largest mission agencies serving the persecuted Church, as a result of his recent arrest Pastor Nadarkhani's small house church has now grown to over 400 people, despite threats of ever increasing violence and further indictment against the church and its leaders.

Not even the fear of death has discouraged this brave group of Iranian Christians to halt their efforts for the sake of Christ. We are reminded by Pastor Nadarkhani and his church that with every underground church that is forcefully disbanded, with every oppressive legislative action against the people of faith, with every pastor thrown in prison, and with every scholarly book promoting the atheistic agenda, the Gospel still stands taller. In each situation, the Church feeds on the very thing that comes against it. With each blow, more and more churches are planted, new pastors are raised up, and bibles and materials are sent all around the globe as God's testament of love for this world. For instance, Gordon-Conwell Theological Seminary recently published a study stating that Christians distribute approximately 83 million bibles annually across the globe. [1] Beyond this, The World Evangelization Research Center estimates that since AD 1500, evangelical Christianity grew from 3 million to over 648 million worldwide today. In fact, it reports that in China alone, despite intense persecution, over 10,000 people a day receive Jesus Christ as their Lord and Savior. [2] Just like in the book of Acts, those persecuting the Gospel discover that "*if it is from God, you will not be able to stop these men; you will only find yourselves fighting against God,*" (Acts 5:39). All over the world, the Gospel shows itself to be unstoppable.

In fact, the only opposition that has any chance of even slowing down this gospel revolution (for nothing can truly stop God's ultimate plans for redemption) is us – the Church. Jesus described this phenomenon best when He said, "*If a kingdom is divided against itself, that kingdom cannot stand,*" (Mark 3:24). Internal division is always our greatest foe, not denominational variations, individuality, or unique distinctions, as these simply bring a greater flavor and perspective to the body of Christ. For example, individual expression says, "This is how I see it," whereas division adds, "This is how I see it, and I can accept no other way than my own." In this, we see the core of divisiveness, which is self-righteousness – a desire to puff ourselves up over those around us. Ideally, the goal should be not to maintain our own perspective and opinion, nor to rise above others around us, but to gain God's perspective. We see this in the Hebrew word for "wait": *qavah*, which means to "bind together," or "intertwine". A New Testament understanding of waiting on the Lord means to allow our perspective to bind together and intertwine with God's perspective, as He transforms our thoughts into His thoughts. Anything less than gaining God's kind of thinking is self-centered and by default breeds division. Perhaps nowhere do we witness the roots of division more than in legalism, as it creeps its way into our thinking and shipwrecks the expression of God's grace in our lives. Legalism stunts the spread of the message and if we are to overcome this foe we must understand it.

Grace Coated Legalism

Legalism, man's attempt at gaining a favorable position with God through external factors, creates divisions by disqualifying others for the purpose of acknowledging or distinguishing one's own qualifications. The stereotypical Pharisee is an obvious example of legalism, and I trust if you've read thus far, the error of the Pharisee is clear to you by now. My guess is that most of us, assuming we've embraced the message of grace, don't spend much time concerning ourselves with personal legalism. Sure we identify legalism in many of the believers around us, but when it comes to ourselves – we're over it, right?

In actuality, unperceived legalism is the most dangerous kind of legalism and I believe for those of us walking in grace, we should concern ourselves deeply with it. One can completely understand the theology of grace, but still operate in law through his thoughts, behaviors, and actions. The disciples themselves even erred in this. In Luke 9, in an attempt to elevate their own position, the disciples argued over which of them was the greatest, tried forcefully to stop others from driving out demons in the name of Christ, and in the end, offered to call down fire from heaven on a Samaritan village, simply for not welcoming Jesus. Now none of us would think of the disciples as legalists, yet here, even in the presence of Christ, as they belittled others in order to elevate themselves, they operated in the very epitome of legalism and self-righteousness – judgment. Judgment questions another's value while inflating your own. As was the case with the disciples, unperceived legalism often hides itself behind what appears to be right motives. Yet, no matter how you look at it, legalism and judgment never exist in the heart of God.

What Did You Call Me?

Several years ago God spoke very clearly to my heart and said to me, "Lucas, you're a snob."

"What did You call me?" I thought. Up until this point, I couldn't remember God ever calling me a name! I was shocked! I quickly retorted, "Lord, I'm a pastor! I love people. I've given my whole life to share good news with the brokenhearted. How can I possibly be a snob?" And with a calmness only God can speak in, and without a hint of condemnation, He said to me, "Lucas, you're a *grace* snob." For a moment I was silent. "Lord, I don't understand. I give grace to everyone. How can I be a snob?" What the Lord said to me next, I'll never forget. "Lucas," He said, "you give grace in abundance to everyone around you, *except* for those who don't believe in grace. To them, you make My grace a law, and condemn them for not giving mercy to others." I was speechless, and I knew He was right. My attitude was preventing the Gospel from doing all that it could in the lives of people around me - even in the lives of the legalists. Sadly, I was still a legalist and didn't even know it.

Swallowed by Grace

To illustrate the legalist trap even further, let's take a look at the life of the Old Testament prophet Jonah. Many of us are familiar with the story of Jonah, a prophet of God called to preach against the great city of Nineveh. Jonah's instructions were fairly simple; go to the people of Nineveh and warn them to repent. Failure to do so would subject Nineveh to the coming calamity. Though the message was straightforward, something about it caused Jonah to flee from his assignment and to seek refuge as far away from Nineveh as he could go. Have you ever wondered *why* it was so difficult for Jonah to obey the Lord's call? I mean, God was calling Jonah to partner with Him in saving an entire city! What a great honor! What was it about Jonah's heart that caused him to flee instead of go? Let's look at Jonah's story a bit more closely.

In the beginning of Chapter Four, we uncover that Jonah was actually angry with God for having shown Nineveh, a known enemy of Israel, mercy! He says,

> "O Lord, is this not what I said when I was still at home? That is why I was so quick to flee to Tarshish. I knew that you are a gracious and compassionate God, slow to anger and abounding in love, a god who relents from sending calamity. Now, O Lord, take away my life, for it is better for me to die than to live."
>
> - Jonah 4:2-3 (NIV)

Incredible, isn't it! Here we see the real reason Jonah fled! Jonah knew that if he spoke against the inhabitants of Nineveh, they would repent and God would have mercy on them. He couldn't bear the thought that the city of Nineveh, an enemy of Israel, might become a recipient of God's love and compassion. Jonah, a prophet of God, refused to extend grace to those he deemed unlovable.

In anger, Jonah embarked upon a journey so far away from God's call, that in the next scene we find him on the first ship out of town. And as we all know, a great storm arose and Jonah admitted that the fierce storm was a result of his disobedience. While the book of Jonah has been utilized for centuries to illustrate the importance of listening to God and obeying His commands, we often miss the reason *why* it was so difficult for Jonah to obey the Lord's call. In fact, Jonah is in such opposition towards God's grace for Nineveh that he would rather die than repent, and keenly agrees to be thrown from the ship.

Jonah is thrown overboard, and the storm ceases after the sea engulfs him. Then, after being swallowed and later spat out onto the shore by a fish, Jonah receives word from the Lord, yet again, to go and preach to Nineveh. This time he wisely chooses to obey. In fact, only when Jonah himself received the abundance of God's grace through the fish that saved his life, did he obey. As Jonah preached, word of his message reached the king of Nineveh. He believed God's messenger and promptly issued a nationwide fast of repentance. As a result, God had mercy on the nation.

Like Jonah, I too had developed limitations around God's goodness that prevented me from loving those I deemed unlovable. The drug addict and the prostitute – for me, they were easy to love. But the Pharisees and the teachers of the law? How could I love them? They knew better! Yet, as I read Romans one morning, the Lord gave me a crystal clear revelation of my own depravity apart from Him, and I cried out for a deeper revelation of His grace. I saw myself for the first time in Paul's words,

> "You, therefore, have no excuse, you who pass judgment on someone else, for at whatever point you judge the other, you are condemning yourself, because you who pass judgment do the same things."
>
> - Romans 2:1 (NIV)

I had developed a silent animosity against legalists, because of the shackles they place on people through their use of fear, manipulation, and standards of performance, and as a result, I too succumbed to legalism, making God's grace into a law and cutting off those whom I had deemed unlovable. I was doing the very same thing I condemned in others.

A Man Named Saul

In the book of Acts, a zealous Pharisee named Saul encountered the God of grace on the road to Damascus and experienced a remarkable life transformation. Like many of us, he abandoned his long held religious traditions and embraced the person of Jesus and the gospel of His grace. It is as powerful a testimony as any, and as many of us know, this man Saul, received a new name, Paul, and became the greatest apostle to ever live. He penned a good majority of the New Testament that we have today, and as history tells us, he eventually died a martyr for Jesus Christ. As Saul, he persecuted Christians, participated in their death, and fought zealously for the destruction of their Gospel. But as Paul, motivated now by the love of God, he planted churches, preached fearlessly, and made it his mission to testify to the gospel of God's grace. But did Paul make this shift from legalism to grace easily? Some might be shocked to see that Paul himself started as a grace snob.

In Acts 9:20-31, immediately after his conversion, Saul "*began to preach in the synagogues that Jesus is the Son of God.*" This passage further tells us that Saul "*grew more and more powerful and baffled the Jews living in Damascus by proving that Jesus is the Christ.*" Furthermore, he "*talked and debated with the Grecian Jesus, but they tried to kill him,*" which I always perceived as senseless persecution towards Saul. What I missed, however, was this key insight,

> "When the brothers learned of this, they took him down to Caesarea and sent him off to Tarsus. Then the church throughout Judea, Galilee and Samaria enjoyed a time of peace. It was strengthened; and encouraged by the Holy Spirit, it grew in numbers, living in the fear of the Lord."
>
> \- Acts 9:30-31 (NIV)

Can you believe it? Saul actually had to be asked to leave, because he ministered God's grace in law! He stirred up so much trouble and insulted so many people in his attempts to prove the message, that the church leaders actually had to send him away in order for the church to grow and prosper in the Lord! Thankfully for all of us, this wasn't the end of Saul's story. We read in Romans 9:2-3, that he eventually became so filled with love for the Pharisees and his fellow Jews that he had a "*great sorrow*" and "*unceasing anguish*" in his heart. He goes on to write that, "*I could wish that I myself were cursed and cut off from Christ for the sake of my brothers, those of my own race.*" Wow! This is *living* grace.

Saul or Jonah?

At the end of his story, Jonah, unlike Saul, sadly concerned himself more with a small vine providing him some temporary shade, than he did with the entire city of Nineveh. Even as a prophet who experienced God's grace firsthand, he had somehow failed to see God's true perspective. He knew grace as a doctrine, but not as a way of life. The same danger exists for us today.

So which person are you? Are you like Jonah, who began his journey with a firsthand revelation of grace only to return to judgmental, legalistic thinking? Or are you like Paul, who was willing to lay down his old ways of forceful argument and debate in order to embrace God's way, which is by love?

The Deciding Factor

In an effort to be heard, I see so many making excuses for throwing stones at legalists. If the message of grace is truly to spark the revolution that we desire, then it must become more than a theological position or an opportunity to prove others wrong. Today, wars are being waged in the name of grace on the battlefields of social medium. This isn't ministry. This is a carnal attempt at calling down fire in order to elevate ourselves. By this, I'm not saying that we shouldn't speak out against manipulation and control, but in doing so we need to extend grace towards those who are still caught in legalism. I'm certain that those zealous for grace will cite Jesus speaking harshly to the Pharisees, and even flipping over the tables in the synagogue, as justification for condemning legalists. But what I see in the Bible is a God who took a zealous legalist like Saul, and flooded his life with so much grace that he was left forever changed. I was Saul. And I often wonder how many people, if given the chance like me, would walk away from a life of law in order to become a person of grace. There are many legalists doing wonderful things for the Lord. We can honor them without honoring everything they believe. To fail to do so, is to continue to be a legalist in disguise – a grace snob. If the Gospel is to go forward, we must abandon every form of legalism, even that which is rooted in grace. We are the deciding factor. The success of the Gospel in our generation rests in our hands.

A Final Word

So where do you stand in the living grace revolution? Do you truly live out grace to everyone you see, or do you withhold grace from those unlovable people who don't deserve it, those legalists who don't believe in grace, who vehemently preach against it? If we want the Gospel to become a revolution that changes the face of the earth, we must *give grace to all,* not just when it's convenient or easy, or because we've had a revelation. If you're reading this book, then chances are you have already come to the conclusion that none of us deserve God's grace. So let none of us withhold it. Brothers and sisters, let us be the example in giving grace, even to those who don't yet believe in grace. Living this life of grace doesn't mean we condone methods of ministry based upon fear and manipulation. It simply means that we choose to see all of God's people from His vantage point.

Grace for the sinner *and* the legalist. This is a grace that will get noticed. This is a grace that will change the world. This is living grace.

> "[25] Now to him who is able to establish you by my gospel and the proclamation of Jesus Christ, according to the revelation of the mystery hidden for long ages past, [26] but now revealed and made known through the prophetic writings by the command of the eternal God, so that all nations might believe and obey him – [27] to the only wise God be glory forever through Jesus Christ! Amen"
>
> - Romans 16:25-27 (NIV)

Endnotes

1. http://christianity.about.com/od/denominations/p/christiantoday.htm
2. http://frontierharvestministries.net/WorldMissionStatistics.dsp

— www.TheLivingGraceProject.com —